Community in Mission

Community in Mission

A Salvationist Ecclesiology

by

Phil Needham

International Headquarters of The Salvation Army
101 Queen Victoria Street, London EC4P 4EP

First published 1987
ISBN 0 85412 526 4

MAJOR PHILIP NEEDHAM, AB, BD, ThM

is a graduate of Miami University, Princeton Theological Seminary and Emory University, and became a Salvation Army officer in 1968. He served as a corps officer (pastor/evangelist) until his appointment in 1971 to the School for Officers' Training, Atlanta, Georgia, where he served successively as Field Training Officer and Chief Side Officer. In 1978 he was appointed back to corps work and later served as divisional secretary, North and South Carolina Division, until his return as principal to the School for Officers' Training, in 1985. Mrs Major Keitha Needham (*née* Holz) shares a partnership ministry with her husband. They have two daughters, Heather and Holly.

Cover by Jim Moss

Printed in Great Britain by
The Campfield Press, St Albans

Contents

Scripture references from the *Revised Standard Version* unless otherwise stated.

Foreword

FOR the first century of its history The Salvation Army was too busily involved in its evangelistic mission to pause and investigate, at any depth, exactly what its form and nature might be within the Church universal. Content to respond to the directives of the Holy Spirit, we concentrated on our work in the world rather than on our role in the Church.

Such questions, however, need to be explored and have taken a significant place in Salvationist thinking in recent years. In this book Major Philip Needham considers Salvationist insights into mission and the community called to maintain that mission in the world.

The biblical basis and the historical context are presented as definitive and explanatory factors in inderstanding a Salvationist theology of redemption and holiness, membership and worship, ministry and renewal. Besides clearly setting out the Salvationist stance on baptism, eucharist and ministry the writer challenges present-day Salvationists to recognise, apply and practice the Army's approach in everyday living and service.

Major Needham was invited to produce a volume which would be a supplement to The Salvation Army's official response to the Lima Document, *Baptism, Eucharist and Ministry*. This book, therefore, is not a theological statement emanating from the deliberations of an official group, but is something more vital—a positive statement from a dedicated Salvationist working from a biblical and experiential perspective.

I believe he has produced a volume which will become a standard work giving a sound and convincing view of The Salvation Army's role and purpose in the Christian Church today.

Eva Burrows.

April 1987.

Introduction

IN the latter part of the 19th century, in England, a Christian missionary* movement came into being. It was born of the conviction of a Methodist couple, William and Catherine Booth, that the churches were failing to bring the gospel of God's love in Christ to the large masses of people—the poor and working classes—and new departures were called for in order to carry out the Great Commission (Matthew 28:19). After repeated attempts to be appointed permanently by the Methodist New Connexion to evangelistic work with the masses, they saw no other alternative outside a courageous embarkment on their own under God's leading.

Where God led them was to the slums of the East End of London. This was the place—more than any other in that great city—of human suffering, exploitation, degradation and immorality. This was London's embarrassment, a festering sore which exposed the social and spiritual diseases of the whole body of the metropolis. This was the place where the Church was surprisingly scarce, given its prominence otherwise in Victorian society—as if it had something on its hands here which it did not quite know how to handle. This was where The Salvation Army began.

The beginning, however, was not the same as the ending. The Booths intended the establishment of an evangelistic organisation for converting the masses to Christ and referring new converts to local churches for membership. To be sure, the campaigns were highly successful: conversions were numerous. But local congregations were not always prepared to accept converted ruffians, riff-raff, derelicts and prostitutes as full members. All they offered, in many churches, were crude benches in the back reserved for those who could not afford pew

*In this book 'missionary' refers to the total outreach of the Church to the world rather than in the more restricted sense of overseas or cross-cultural evangelism only.

rental and needed to be kept separate from the more civilised, dues-paying members. The Victorian Church had its own version of the Pauline 'dividing wall of hostility' (Ephesians 2:14). The Booths' impoverished converts could see the wall very clearly, and feel it very deeply. They were not wanted.

It was inevitable—and perhaps right—that they return to those through whose ministry and care they had come to new birth in Christ. The Booths found themselves inundated with Christians without a fellowship. Their Salvationist movement was now standing at a new crossroads. An important decision had to be made: either to continue working with existing congregations to find a way for converts of humble estate to be accepted and trained as members, or, to embark on yet another significant departure by allowing that this new evangelistic movement would also be the permanent spiritual home of those converts who felt led to make it such and who themselves wanted to become involved in its mission. Based on experience, the first option seemed unpromising. The choice—made prayerfully and wisely—was to be the second.

The Booths now had a church on their hands. A very unchurchly church, to be sure; a church which did not like to be *called* a 'church'—remember, 'church' was associated with bad memories, discrimination, rejection—but a church which bore all the essential marks of the body of Christ. Whom the respectable Victorian churches were unable to embrace, the Salvationists welcomed home, and in this new fellowship of believers, sharing a common experience and united in a common mission, the Lord found more rock upon which to build his Church.

The Salvation Army—as this movement came to be called in 1878—is as much an integral part of the one true catholic (universal) Christian Church as is any other denomination or ecclesiastical tradition. In the early days, many would have taken issue with such a statement—and did. In this day of ecumenical enlightenment, those who take issue would probably be accused of ecclesiastical arrogance. The true body of Christ is united in the essentials and mutually tolerant on other matters. The Salvation Army claims total allegiance to that which the Scriptures clearly show to be essential to Christian faith and practice.

On the other hand, it has no right to claim ecclesiastical superiority. Like any other denomination, it has its strengths and weaknesses. It has not always maintained its missionary commitment, and it has at times been guilty of spiritual Phariseeism. It has sometimes displayed an isolationist and sectarian spirit. And it has suffered some of the deadly consequences of creeping institutionalisation. The Salvation Army is no better—or worse—than its sister fellowships in Christ.

It does, however, have an important contribution to make to the Church as a whole. The very reason for the Army's emergence in Victorian England and its consequent rapid spread around the world, is a clarion reminder to the churches of their calling in the world. The Army came into being because—allowing for some glorious exceptions—by and large, the churches were not carrying out their mission to the poor and dispossessed. If one of the signs that the Kingdom had come in Jesus the Christ was that the poor had the gospel preached to them (Matthew 11:5), the Victorian churches had forgotten. The Army reminded them.

It stands *today* as a reminder. Only now it needs to remind *itself* more than anyone else. It could lose its own missionary heartbeat. It could forget that the sole reason for its existence is the world for whom Christ died. Nothing would be more pale and pathetic than a missionary movement without a mission.

Hence, this Salvationist ecclesiology[1] is written primarily for The Salvation Army. It is written with the conviction that the Salvationist movement has embodied key characteristics of the Church and its calling in the world, and in the hope that these characteristics, when understood, will give Salvationists today a vision of the missionary future into which their Lord is leading them. But it is also written for the whole Church as a basis for theological reflection upon the Salvationist movement itself, but primarily as a perspective on ecclesiology as a whole. Salvationist history has something to say to the Church.

One thing should be made very clear at the outset: this is *not* an ecclesiology of The Salvation Army but a Salvationist ecclesiology. The Salvation Army is only one concrete expression of the Church in human history; it is also a human institution which is subject to many of the forces and influences to which all institutions are subject. To write an ecclesiology of this one ecclesiastical expression would be idolatrous, a substitution of the part for the whole. Any attempt at a true ecclesiology assumes that a theology of the Church universal is intended.

This is not to say that a true ecclesiology cannot be historically conditioned; all of theology is. Every Christian generation needs an ecclesiology which is both faithful to the gospel as revealed in the Scriptures and attentive to the particular historical context in which it finds itself. A true ecclesiology finds its source in the Scriptures and its thrust in the hopes and challenges of the social context. It must speak both with authority and to the times. Unless it does both it is of little use.

Each generation provides its peculiar challenges to the life and mission of the Church. In responding to those challenges, the Church searches the Scriptures and its faith and inevitably rediscovers aspects of its life and calling which need to be taken more seriously in the light of the present situation. In this way historical circumstances stimulate the recovery of neglected areas of ecclesiology.

The Salvation Army came into being in an era when the urban Church was, for the most part, neglecting its missionary calling. The social, economic and spiritual alienation of the poor masses cried out to the Church for response, but few heard. The early Salvationists were among the few who did. The cry drove them to rediscover the pre-eminence of mission in the work of the New Testament Church, and out of this rediscovery The Salvation Army came into being.

Hence a peculiarly *Salvationist* ecclesiology necessarily reflects this prejudice toward the Church's missionary calling. It could never be seen as an ecclesiology for the whole Church, for no other reason than the fact that Salvationist history and experience have created a selection of emphases and priorities which would not be shared by all Christian fellowships. But this is not the same as saying that Salvationists hold tenets that deviate from universally accepted and scripturally supported doctrines held in common by most Christians. On the contrary, The Salvation Army claims that all its eleven doctrines are in keeping with the Church's historic faith and practice founded upon the teachings and emphases of the Scriptures. Thus, the ecclesiology which is here being written finds its basis in the Scriptures and its uniqueness in historic Salvationist mission. Such an ecclesiology is a worthwhile enterprise because, first, Salvationists need to understand why their fellowship was called into being and how it can continue to be faithful to its calling and, second, a Salvationist ecclesiology stands as a reminder to the Church that its mission in the world is primary, and that the life of the Church ought largely to be shaped by a basic commitment to mission.

How, then, will a Salvationist ecclesiology that is scripturally based and missionally biased unfold? From a Salvationist perspective, how are we to understand who the people of God are and what their purpose in the world is? The answer is that we will seek to develop this ecclesiology under six headings which can be considered the essential[2] realities constituting the true Church. They can be expressed in the following phrases:

Chartered by Christ—The new humanity
Created by the Holy Spirit—The redemptive fellowship
Called to a journey—The pilgrim people
Commissioned for battle—The army of salvation
Encamped for renewal—The nurturing community
Committed to the future—The colony of hope.

In these descriptions we see all that the Church is. Everything that must be said about the Church is rooted in the realities to which they point. These are the foundations of our ecclesiology.

1

Chartered by Christ

The new humanity

The Church is a community which comes into being in response to the Kingdom of God through faith in Jesus the Christ as the one in whom the Kingdom is realised.

JESUS came preaching the Kingdom of God. By this term he meant both the establishment of God's rule in human life—individual and corporate—and the amazing consequences of accepting this rule. The consequences were a reversal of the relationships characteristic of a fallen world order—for example, love not only of friends but also of enemies (Matthew 5:43-47), unlimited forgiveness of others (Luke 17:3, 4), service over status (Mark 10:42-45).

The gospel is the good news that in Jesus this Kingdom is now present and accessible (Luke 7:22; 17:21), that all of history is moving toward the Kingdom's full realisation in a transcendant order (Revelation 21:1-4), and that through faith in Jesus as the Christ (the Messiah of God) the Kingdom may be entered (ie, salvation received) and a new life begun (Galatians 3:26; Ephesians 2:8). Through his voluntary death on the cross (John 10:18), the incomparable act of self-giving love, Jesus released power enough to bring this salvation into the world (1 Corinthians 1:17, 18) and to reconcile fallen humanity to himself (Colossians 1:20)—ie, power enough to establish the Kingdom as a reality in human life. Through his resurrection from the dead, he demonstrated the Kingdom's triumph in the cross and gave the promise of its completion in human life and history (1 Peter 1:3-9).

How the new humanity in Christ begins

This gospel is the starting point for the Church. The Church comes into being when the gospel is received—that is, when persons accept and enter the Kingdom through faith in Jesus. It is the fellowship of those who believe in Jesus as the Christ sent from God to heal the brokenness of human life and restore lost fellowship with God and man. It is the community of those who are bound together by a common faith in Jesus. We call this community 'the new humanity' because it is based upon that which contradicts and supersedes the old, fallen humanity; it is, in fact, a new order of life based upon the gospel.

Because Jesus as the Christ is the one through whom the Kingdom is entered and realised, we speak of the Church as the community which is 'chartered by Christ'. He is the one who delivers the Kingdom to the faithful and grants all the privileges, rights, protections and powers which life in the Kingdom entails. He is the Lord of the Church, and the Church therefore lives in obedience to him. This obedience defines the Church's life and action under Jesus' lordship. The Church has a bias toward obedience rather than observance because of this lordship.[3] It is called not to perpetuate ritual but to step out in trusting obedience to its Lord's commands. Discipleship is the Church's way of life. The Church looks to its Lord not only as its Saviour from the Kingdom of sin and death, but also as the source of authority and the norm of conduct in the new Kingdom. As the reliable, Spirit-inspired witness to Christ as the Word of God, the initiator of this new Kingdom and the Lord of life, the Scriptures are the written authority and norm for Christian faith and practice, and therefore for all ecclesiology.

In obedience to its Lord, the Church goes into all the world preaching the gospel (Mark 16:15, alternate ending) and attempting to make disciples of all nations (Matthew 28:19): its starting point is a *universal* gospel. The privilege of the Kingdom is for the whosoever (John 3:16). This means, of course, that citizenship in the Kingdom is freely chosen. The Kingdom is entered by faith, and since faith is the only act without merit, it is possible for *any* true seeker after God. The universal gospel implies entrance into the Kingdom as a free choice.

How the new humanity in Christ is celebrated and nurtured

In order for there to be true unity in the (universal) gospel, there must be freedom in the diversity of culturally conditioned forms, rituals, ceremonies and governments in the Church as a whole. The strength of the universal gospel is that '. . . it is the power of God for salvation to *everyone* who has faith, to the Jew first and also to the Greek' (Romans 1:16). In order to protect this universality, the Church must allow for considerable diversity in the expression and nurture of faith, so that acceptance of the gospel does not depend upon simultaneous acceptance of a particular culture or ecclesiastical tradition and thereby nullify the universality. It is a disservice to the gospel to insist that grace must be received through the mediation of a particular ritual or procedure, and there is no evidence in the New Testament from which a case can be argued for such a view. Grace is immediate and accessible. When the Word became flesh, God's grace appeared for the salvation of all men (Titus 2:11), 'and from his fullness have we all received, grace upon grace' (John 1:16). 'Each one of us . . . has been given his own share of grace, given as Christ allotted' (Ephesians 4:7, *JB*).

The immediacy of grace, however, does not require the elimination of sacred rites. Man has a need to nurture and celebrate profound spiritual realities through symbolic acts. A Gnostic disparagement of palpable symbols and rituals which communicate through the senses is, or borders on, Christian heresy. What the immediacy of grace does imply is that no ritual can be seen as somehow necessary in order for someone to receive grace and that *any* ritual which faithfully conveys the gospel and adequately allows for response is appropriate. Each Christian fellowship is therefore free to develop those symbolic acts which best nurture and celebrate a response to the gospel which is attentive to the social, cultural and historical context of its life and mission. Such freedom is necessary if the free grace of God is to be accepted by the Church and prescribed rituals in particular traditions not understood as the requisite means of experiencing that grace.

What, then, are the criteria for those rites which evoke and reinforce the reality of the Church as the new humanity chartered by Christ? The criteria are in fact those significant aspects of this reality which ought to be communicated in the rite. We list them as follows:

The new humanity in Christ comes about through entrance into a totally new reality, the Kingdom of God now present in human life.

It involves a change in life patterns and goals.

This change is made possible through personal repentance and divine forgiveness.

Jesus the Christ is the one through whom this forgiveness is offered and effected.

Since he is also the one who is Lord in the new Kingdom, citizenship (discipleship) requires obedience to him and emulation of him.

Personal response to Jesus as Saviour, Lord and pattern is made in freedom.

Becoming a part of the new humanity in Christ is a step which should be recognised and celebrated publicly as a witness (Matthew 10:32).

It has the character of enlisting in an army, the discipline of which is necessary in enduring the hardship of living in the new Kingdom in the midst of a fallen and opposing world order.

In addition to conveying these aspects of the new humanity in Christ, the rite ought also to celebrate the immediacy of grace. Nothing in it ought to imply that grace is automatically prescribed or purveyed through the performance of the rite itself. Rather, the rite must be a celebration of the immediacy of grace to those who are the active participants. When a rite loses this celebratory and spontaneous character, it is near to becoming a peremptory ritual which claims to control and channel grace. In no way can a rite effect salvation; in no way can saving grace be received representationally.

Most Christian fellowships celebrate entrance into the new Kingdom through Christ by means of the rite of water baptism.[4] Baptism is seen by these fellowships as a 'rite of passage' signifying entrance into new life through Jesus Christ and union of the one baptised with Christ and with his people. The significance of the rite is drawn from Scripture references which associate baptism with important dimensions of conversion to Christ: participation in Christ's death and resurrection (Romans 6:3-5; Colossians 2:12); a washing away of sin (1 Corinthians 6:11); a new birth (John 3:5); an enlightenment by Christ

(Ephesians 5:14); a clothing in Christ (Galatians 3:27); a renewal by the Spirit (Titus 3:5); the experience of salvation from the flood (1 Peter 3:20, 21); an exodus from bondage (1 Corinthians 10:1, 2); and a liberation into a new humanity in which barriers of division whether of sex or race or social status are transcended (Galatians 3:27, 28; 1 Corinthians 12:13).[5]

A Salvationist ecclesiology affirms these dimensions of conversion. It also acknowledges that water baptism was adopted by a major part of the New Testament Church as a rite which had both the potential to evoke suggestions of these spiritual dimensions and precedent in both Jewish and pagan cultural practice. But it also avers that neither Jesus nor the apostles intended to establish that particular rite as an *indispensable* part of true Spirit baptism,[6] and that readings of scriptural references to 'baptism' as a spiritual experience, that see water baptism as a necessary component of the event, are theologically unjustifiable.

Water baptism, then, cannot stand on its own—no more than can any other religious rite. It is no more than a sign of an inner experience, and without the independent reality of the inner event, the rite is a mere form. The sign of baptism can be a very effective witness to the world of the transformation wrought by faith if, in fact, the evidence supports the claim. It reinforces the convert in his new commitment, and it reminds the gathered fellowship of the commitments they have made. Rich in the symbolism of death and resurrection, a washing away, cleansing, rebirth and renewal, it is a fitting representation and confirmation of the conversion that has taken place.

But it is not the only public witness to this spiritual reality. The Salvationist fellowship has its own rites of public witness to conversion. When the gospel is preached in Salvation Army meetings (services of worship), persons are invited to respond by coming forward and kneeling at a mercy seat (a place of prayer), thereby signifying their penitence, desire for conversion, and personal resolve. The symbolism of this action is reminiscent of Jesus' frequent call for would-be disciples to step out, leave what they have and follow him (see Luke 9:57-62). The kneeling at the mercy seat points to the true humility of those who see the inadequacy and shame of their life outside discipleship, and the longing to be converted to true discipleship through spiritual death and resurrection. Through faith the seeker rises from the mercy seat a new person in Jesus Christ (2 Corinthians 5:17).

There is, of course, no guarantee of conversion by virtue of the act of coming to the mercy seat, nor is this regarded as an essential precondition of membership. The coming forward is only a sign that a search is in progress and conversion is contemplated. As such, it strengthens the seeker and elicits the support of the congregation in concerned prayer. In actuality, the mercy seat itself is symbolic of *any place* where a seeker after God comes in prayer. The true mercy seat is of the heart, and the outward act of kneeling at a prayer bench, or any other place, is nothing if not the outward sign of the kneeling soul.

The new convert is prepared for soldiership (membership) during a period of time as a recruit. Then he is enrolled as a soldier in a public ceremony. This enrolment or swearing-in signifies an important dimension of response to the new Kingdom through faith in Jesus: it stresses *discipleship.* Having entered the Kingdom, the convert becomes a disciple who follows Jesus as Lord and patterns his life accordingly. The soldier enrolment makes clear that discipleship is the purpose of conversion, and it celebrates the convert's acceptance of this calling by utilising the military metaphor of enlistment into a life of spiritual discipline and warfare (Ephesians 6:11-17; 1 Timothy 6:12; 2 Timothy 2:3, 4). The convert is enrolled as a soldier under the flag of The Salvation Army whose pattern and colours are symbolic of the redeeming blood of Christ, the refining and empowering fire of the Holy Spirit, and the purity of God and of those who singlemindedly serve him. Again, the ceremony of itself has no efficaciousness apart from the integrity and seriousness of the convert who is taking the step.[7]

It should be noted that in The Salvation Army *young persons* can be enrolled as junior soldiers. There is no requirement that a person must reach young adulthood before he is capable of discipleship. Rather, since Jesus used the trusting attitude of little children as analogous to religious faith (Mark 10:14, 15), the Army allows children to make a faith response and to be enrolled as soldiers. As such they are nurtured in the faith, and they serve according to their abilities and maturity.

Summary

Let us now summarise the contributions of Salvationist ecclesiology to an understanding of the Church as the new humanity chartered by Christ. Here are the doctrines emphasised by the Salvationist movement.[8]

First, the Church is comprised of *those who have received and give witness to the immediacy of God's grace in Jesus Christ.* The Kingdom is received through faith, and this faith saves quite apart from rituals and ecclesiastical prescriptions. The new humanity takes its stand in the accessibility of saving grace over against all attempts to mediate grace through office or ritual. Along with the Society of Friends (Quakers), The Salvation Army witnesses to the whole Church that in Christ the saving grace of God is accessible to the whosoever and efficacious for all who have faith in Christ irrespective of office or ritual.[9]

Second, all who have entered God's Kingdom of grace share *one baptism of the Holy Spirit and one obedience to Jesus Christ.* The new humanity in Christ is a unified body, and this corporate unity consists of a shared status through spiritual baptism and a shared mission under the command of Jesus Christ.[10] Hence, the basis for Christian unity can never be uniformity or even similarity of government, ritual, or claims to historic apostolic succession. Christians are truly united in their spiritual baptism, quite apart from the specific ritual that is followed in order to express and celebrate this conversion; and in their commitment to obey the missionary Christ while affirming the unique missionary strengths of different Christian fellowships. There is no other basis for Christian unity. This is clear when we view the varieties of ritual practice among those who accept Jesus as Lord.

Third, entrance into the Kingdom and participation in the new humanity in Christ are synonymous with *accepting the challenge of discipleship.* Conversion in the initial sense is not an end in itself. It is that beginning experience of divine love, acceptance and forgiveness which frees the convert to realise his potential in Christ by becoming a disciple. Discipleship is the corollary of confessing Jesus as Lord. It is the means by which the Church pursues its calling and carries out its mission in the world. It is obedience to Jesus Christ, and, as such, the way of life of the new humanity. There is no other way to participate in the Kingdom.

Fourth, *the rituals of the Church*—whether spontaneous or institutionalised—*are signs of spiritual events, celebrations of God's grace in human life, and witnesses to God's transforming presence.* They *point* to divine reality. They are not themselves that reality, nor do they somehow effect the work of grace. They can be spiritually illuminating and often elicit an overwhelming sense of God's presence, but that is the case only when they are performed in response to the gracious work of God in human life, and as a symbolic witness to what God has in fact wrought. Rituals such as water baptism or soldier enrolment effect nothing.[11] They are outward, symbolic expressions of spiritual transformation. They are the witness of a community which has come into being in response to the Kingdom of God through faith in Jesus the Christ as the one in whom the Kingdom is realised.

2

Created by the Holy Spirit

The redemptive fellowship

The Church is a fellowship created by the Holy Spirit in which those who have responded to the Kingdom of God through faith are empowered to live redemptive lives.

THE Church is not the Kingdom of God. It is that community which comes into being in *response* to the Kingdom. It is that community which receives the Kingdom and reorders its life in the light of the Kingdom's dawning. As the community which has been chartered by Christ to live in the reality of the new Kingdom, how does the Church realise itself? How does it *become* what it is? What enables it to actualise the promise of the Kingdom in human life?

The answer is that the Church is actually created by the Holy Spirit. The unity of believers in fellowship and service is the Holy Spirit's work. It is the Holy Spirit who empowers a diverse group of converts to come together into a fellowship that lives redemptively and, by so doing, intimates and illustrates the Kingdom that has come in Christ. Nothing other than Holy Spirit power creates the Church.

How the Kingdom is expressed in the Church

What exactly does the Holy Spirit create when he creates the

Church? How is the Kingdom expressed in the life of the Church through the Holy Spirit? There are four characteristics of this expression.

First, the Spirit creates *a visible expression of the peace that has been made in Christ.* When the early Spirit-empowered Church 'met constantly to hear the apostles teach, and to share the common life (*koinonia*), to break bread, and to pray' (Acts 2:42, *NEB*), they were, through the Spirit's power, visibly expressing the reality that in Christ divided men had become 'one new man . . . one body through the cross, thereby bringing the hostility to an end' (Ephesians 2:15, 16). By allowing the Spirit to create unity, the Church demonstrates its attentiveness to Jesus' prayer for them: '[I pray] that they may all be one; even as thou, Father, art in me, and I in thee, that they also may be in us, so that the world may believe that thou hast sent me' (John 17:21). Clearly, the credibility of the gospel is dependent upon the unity of those who in response to the gospel have allowed the Spirit to break through their dividing walls. Hence the apostle Paul utilises the analogy of the human body to illustrate the Church as a unity of diverse parts which work together empathetically for a common end, the growth and health of the body (Romans 12:2-8; 1 Corinthians 12:4-31). This body of Christ is the 'new creation' in Christ by which the redeemed are 'changed . . . from enemies into his friends . . .' (2 Corinthians 5:18, *GNB*). In the power of the Spirit, reconciled living becomes possible.

Second, the Spirit creates *a community of shared life.* The Church is not a grouping of individual Christians; it is a community in which Christians share in one another's struggles and hopes. In the fellowship of believers, Christians bear one another's burdens (Galatians 6:2), weep together, rejoice together (Romans 12:15), lift one another up in prayer (Romans 1:9; 2 Corinthians 9:14; Ephesians 1:16; Philippians 1:4; Colossians 4:2; etc), and love one another as Christ loved them (John 13:34). There is a togetherness in this fellowship that goes far deeper than mere camaraderie. The pledge which the Spirit empowers the Church to carry out is the pledge of members of the community of faith to *be with* one another in *every* circumstance.[12]

Third, the Spirit creates *a high level of participation in the fellowship.* In affirming the diversity of gifts within the Church, the apostle Paul charges members to participate in the life of the community by putting their gifts to use: 'Having gifts that differ according to the grace given to us, let us *use* them . . .' (Romans 12:6). This utilisation of the gifts of each member is made possible through one of the Spirit's most important endowments: genuine appreciation for one another's uniqueness as essential for the balance of the whole. In the Christian fellowship, persons who are very different from one another can work together because they believe that 'to *each* is given the manifestation of the Spirit for the common good' (1 Corinthians 12:7). A Spirit-empowered fellowship achieves a high level of participation because members appreciate the special way in which the Spirit manifests himself through the uniqueness and gifts of each member (1 Corinthians 12:14 ff).

One of the most important areas of participation in the fellowship is the decision-making process. In the early Church, decision making was neither highly structured nor done in isolation. It involved the community.[13] As time went on and the priesthood developed, however, diversity of gifts was depreciated. The clergy were seen to be concerned with the spiritual, the laity with the secular. Hence, clerical privilege and power expanded. The result was a considerable diminution of lay participation in the life and decision making of the Church. From time to time in the history of the Church, movements such as lay monasticism and the Protestant Reformation have made attempts to restore the laity to their rightful place, but the dilemma is still with us. The life and mission of the Church always suffer where the power and wisdom of the people of God are not at work in the fellowship. The Spirit does not create a fellowship in which participation and decision making are concentrated in a few. The Spirit creates a living organism in which every part is contributory to the whole.

Fourth, the Spirit creates a community which seeks to *simplify life.* Simplicity of living enables Christians to free themselves from confusing distractions and compulsive busyness—that is, from pursuits which serve to distract from their spiritual pilgrimage. It enables them to address the important issues of life and to give attention to the spiritual commonwealth which they have entered and which is the focus of their pilgrimage. As such it serves as an invitation to others to cultivate their lives and their relationships in some depth. And finally, it is a requirement for the mobility and adaptability which the mission of the Church requires.[14] This ability to focus on the essentials and to withstand the temptation to be pulled into diversionary entanglements and unworthy pursuits, is given by the Spirit to those who are living their lives in response to the Kingdom.

Having described in this summary way what the Spirit creates when he creates the Church, let us also point out emphatically that the community of believers is called to demonstrate the interpersonal and social relationships which are the goal for *all* of humanity. In response to the Kingdom which has come in Christ, the Church exemplifies—albeit imperfectly—the fulfilment of human life in community. What the Spirit makes possible for the Church, God intends for all mankind.

Hence, the Church is called by God to invite the world, the larger community, to the fellowship of the Kingdom of God through Christ. In doing so, it seeks faithfully to live in response to the Kingdom itself, lays claim to its own gospel-given resources for the development of community, boldly proclaims and demonstrates the meaning of community in Christ, and offers itself as a welcoming community to those who live in personal isolation. If the world today is searching for community,[15] the Church is inviting it to find community in the fellowship of those who have been reconciled to God and man and are now empowered by the Spirit to live redemptively with one another in the world.

How the Holy Spirit empowers the Church

We now come to a very important matter. We have described the nature of the (Church) community which the Holy Spirit creates, and we have asserted that this community is an expression of the social life which God purposes for all persons. The statement at the beginning of this chapter asserts that the end result of what the Spirit creates in the Church is the power to live *redemptive* lives. What do we mean by this power?

Before answering this question, we must first point out that the *Church* is God's purposeful setting for freeing Christians to live redemptively. It is in a community where persons have been reconciled to God and one another, where life is shared, where participation is valued and all gifts are appreciated, and where the focus of life is on matters of eternal significance, that redemptive living becomes possible. Redemption is the repossession of that which is of value. Those who have been reconciled can cease fighting battles that have no real victories and can get on with repossessing those experiences and concerns and relationships which hold promise. Those who share life in the Church community are repossessing the blessing of human fellowship, which sin is constantly at work to undermine. Those who experience the acceptance of their participation and the appreciation of their special gifts within the fellowship are repossessing their self-worth and the value of their contribution to the lives of others. Those who have simplified life in order to focus on the essentials are repossessing eternity. The Church is the place where the Spirit makes this repossession an exciting possibility.

We now see that redemptive living is what the Spirit-created Church frees the Christian to pursue. We also see that redemptive living is the process of repossessing that which God gives to life and sin seeks to extort. How then can we best describe this redemptive living? What kind of life does the Spirit empower the Church to repossess.

First, the Spirit empowers the Church to repossess the *sacramental life.* Whereas we are opposed to the idea of any formal sacrament as a means of salvation, we are deeply committed to the sacramental life as that which salvation through faith in Christ makes possible. In the early years of the Salvationist movement, William Booth described this new life by deritualising the language of the Lord's supper:

> Let us remember him who died for us continually. Let us remember his love every hour of our lives, and continually feed on him—not on Sunday only, and then forget him all the week, but let us by faith eat his flesh and drink his blood continually: and 'whatsoever you do, whether you eat or drink, do all to the glory of God'.[16]

The sacramental life is based on the continuity of God's incarnational presence in all human biography and history. It aims at living in a way that imbibes this Real Presence and gives witness to it. In this context there can be no sacraments divorced from everyday life; there can only be the sacramental potential of each moment of everyday life. This was how Horatius Bonar put it:

> So shall no part of day or night
> From sacredness be free;
> But all my life, in every step,
> Be fellowship with thee.[17]

In keeping with its Wesleyan heritage, The Salvation Army has traditionally used the word 'holiness' to describe the sacramental life, and 'sanctification' as the gracious act of God which makes holiness possible. The New Testament clearly teaches that Jesus gave his life on the cross so that righteousness could become a living possibility for those who responded in faith to this supreme act of divine, self-giving love (Romans 8:3, 4; Hebrews 13:12; 1 Peter 2:24; 1 John 3:5, 8). Hence, the apostle Paul and others boldly proclaim the death of the 'old man' (Romans 6:6, *AV*), the elimination of any claim the 'lower nature' had on us (8:12), the acquisition of a 'new nature' (Colossians 3:9, 10), the sanctification of life (1 Corinthians 6:11; Hebrews 10:10, 12-14), the state of holiness (1 Thessalonians 5:23; 1 Peter 2:9)—all for those who respond in faith to the God who was in Christ. This new life in the Spirit, or holiness of life, is God's will for his people (1 Thessalonians 4:3) and a reflection of his ownership (Leviticus 11:45; 1 Peter 1:15, 16). It can also be described as the sacramental life.

The sacramental life is lived in the power of the Spirit. Those who 'walk by the Spirit' look for the sacredness of every moment, the presence of God in every encounter, the divine possibility in every human soul, the sacrament in every experience. They shun the compromise and accommodation of sacred here and secular there: they look for God *everywhere.* They may not 'see' him everywhere, but they know he is there, and they pray for better eyesight! They believe in Incarnation.

We contend that the sacramental life is a repossession, through Christ and in the power of the Holy Spirit, of God's original and enduring intention for human existence. The Genesis account of the Fall describes the beginning in human history of that great rift which is the consequence of sin. Out of that rift come other divisions, as sin seeps into the vulnerable crevices of a fallen race. Perhaps the most insidious division, which at times has reached the proportions of a gaping canyon, is between that in life which is considered sacred and that which is not, between that which is defined as holy by nature and that which is irrevocably consigned to the realm of profane, between that part of personal life which is seen as concerned with serious discipleship and that which is not. The sacramental life is lived on the premise that all such 'dividing walls' have been broken down in the cross, that all of life is now sacred and should be celebrated as such, that holiness is the freedom to live every moment in God's presence.

The second repossession which the Spirit makes possible is *life together.* We have already made note of the importance of reconciliation through Christ's death, through which *koinonia*, the Church's shared life, becomes a reality. Let it also be noted that a serious consequence of the Fall is the loss of fellowship—with both God and other human beings. Human beings are not only driven from the garden (Genesis 3:24), never to return again to the sublime relationship with God which it symbolised, they also live henceforth at enmity with one another (4:15). This loss of human fellowship is an agonising strand that runs through Old Testament history, with illustration after illustration of hurt, unfaithfulness, tragedy and brutality in every area of social life. It characterised the world into which Jesus was born. It contributed to his crucifixion.

But here's the irony. The New Testament proclaims that Jesus' crucifixion put an end to this enmity, and *yet* his first-generation Church is torn by divisions of its own: Jew and Gentile, rich and poor, this party and that. And it hasn't ended yet. Will it ever?

It *will* surely end when the Kingdom is consummated in human history and the 'former things' have passed away (Revelation 21:4). But what about the present? Is the Church to wring its hands in despair, acquiesce in the inevitability of man's inhumanity to man—even within the fellowship of believers—and govern its relationships under the safety and protection of the law? Can grace not abound in our life together?

The answer is that it can and does. Christ suffered and died to restore unity to a world fragmented by sin. The apostle Paul spoke of him as the One through whom God was reconciling the world to himself (2 Corinthians 5:18, 19). He is the one in whom all things are to be united (Colossians 1:20; Ephesians 1:9, 10). Hence, reconciliation through Christ must continue to work itself out in history, and the Church is called upon to participate in this reconciling work. This participation has little to do with the laws and organisation and programmes of the Church; it has everything to do with experiencing the grace of God in the life of the fellowship. Only as the Church allows the grace of God to bring reconciliation in the fellowship does the gospel of grace which it proclaims in the world have credibility. The God who calls his Church to a life of reconciliation is not mocking his people. He is not calling them to that for which he does not empower them. In Christ peace *has* come and enmity *is* ended. The Church can be defined as the society of those who have accepted the peace treaty and are learning step by step how to live at peace with God and man. We say 'step by step' because the ways of enmity linger insidiously and are so ingrained in human relationships that the new ways of peace must be tried out one risk at a time, and sometimes there is a good bit of clumsy stumbling and trial-and-error. But where there is genuine acceptance through faith of the peace that is in Christ, the Church is moving decisively beyond enmity.

The Church, then, is the fellowship of believers-in-the-peace. It is the people who have been reconciled who know, and experience in significant ways, peace with God, themselves and their neighbours. For them, the decisive battle is over; they operate on the assumption that in Christ God has reconciled the world to himself. Both their life together and their missionary involvement in the world are based upon this assumption. When the second-century Christian apologist, Athenagoras, said that Christians followed the practice of not striking back when struck, of not suing when robbed, of giving when asked and of loving their neighbours as themselves,[18] he was describing attitudes and actions which characterised the Christ who was now incarnate in the life of the Church (1 Peter 2:21-23). The same could be said of many of the early-day Salvationists who were subjected to scorn, derision, abuse and open attack, but blessed their enemies.

The Church, then, is not only the society in Christ which is repossessing the integrity of sacramental living, it is also a society which is repossessing the peace of the human community which sin seeks to shatter. In the unfolding life of the Church, the Spirit frees Christians to restore the lost bond of love and mutual affirmation. As a fellowship of reconciliation, the Church is in the process of becoming.

Third, the Spirit empowers the Church to live *life for others.* It is clear that God chose servanthood as the form of his reconciling mission in the world (Philippians 2:5-8). Therefore, his Christ, the one through whom that mission was to be carried out, became a servant. The source of Christ's servanthood was to be found in his radical obedience to God (Matthew 26:39; Mark 14:36; Luke 22:42); and its focus was persons (Matthew 20:28; Mark 10:45).

Hence, Christ served men, but at the same time was obedient only to the Father. He was servant of all, but slave only to God. He was servant of all without doing what everyone wished. In fact he could be servant of all *only* by his obedience to the One who sent him. The higher obedience made possible an inclusive service: the reality of Christ's servanthood is that it was lived for all mankind, the true family of God, with no exceptions, because its source was obedience to the impartial Father. When God 'emptied himself' in Christ (Philippians 2:7), he set himself to offer a redemptive alternative to self-serving lifestyles and bigoted religion. He became a slave who was totally obedient to the Father and a servant who was fully available to the human race.

This radical obedience and this loving availability came together powerfully in the cross. The world does not understand the cross because the cross is the potent symbol of God's servant way, which, to a power-hungry world, seems foolish (1 Corinthians 1:18-25). But to the Church, it represents the true character of life and mission. As the embodiment of Christ's radical obedience to the Father and his servant love for all humanity, it becomes the norm for the Church's servant calling (John 13:34, 35; 15:12, 13; Philippians 2:1-8; Ephesians 4:1-3, 5:2; 1 John 3:16-18).

Servant love is the other side of radical obedience and is inseparable from it. It is possible, in other words, only where God is being obeyed. The Church is free to live its life for others because it is not torn in many directions; it obeys only God. Hence, singularity of obedience frees the Church for servant love.

It is God who calls the Church to servant love and who in the crucified Christ provides the model for that love; and what he calls the Church to, the Holy Spirit empowers it to possess. In Christ the new reality has triumphed, the reality that peace has come and that all manifestations of enmity are *un*-reality: they have no basis and place in the new Kingdom. Through the power of the Holy Spirit, the Church takes the risk of living by the peace, meeting enmity with love, living for one another. It does so imperfectly, and sometimes its actions belie its claim to a reconciled life and a servant calling: the former life patterns often persist and accommodation to society brings susceptibility to influences which are absorbed from the old destructive order which, while passing away, is still pervasive. But the Church, with all its shortcomings, is still the society of those who have received the Kingdom in Christ and are called by God and empowered by the Spirit to live the Kingdom's reality and by doing so, to repossess the incredible possibilities for human life of which sin would deprive every person.

In the midst of a world drenched with enmity, the Church is that society of persons who take their stand where enmity was robbed of its power (the cross) and who serve one another in love through the power of the Spirit. Servant love is the way of life for those who are at peace with God and man; it is the only way to proliferate the reconciliation which has come in Christ. It is also the way of the sacramental life; when God's presence is recognised to be everywhere and his will the object of every action, there is absolutely no place for self-importance and self-service, and with these being so totally out of place, love of God and man is understood to be what it really is: the only way to live redemptively in society.

How the Church celebrates and nurtures the redemptive character of its fellowship

As a redemptive fellowship created and empowered by the Holy Spirit, how does the Church celebrate and nurture those realities which we have described?

First, let us consider the sacramental life. Undoubtedly in the Church the most prevalent celebration of sacramental living is the Lord's supper. Interpretations of the significance of the supper range from the memorial feast (a feast of remembrance) to the highly institutionalised sacrament which is considered in and of itself a means of saving grace. Few scholars would say that the institution of the Lord's supper as a sacrament has clear scriptural foundation.[19] What is clear is that Jesus' last meal with his disciples was fraught with spiritual meaning, and he knew and intended that it be remembered as such.[20] They had shared many meals together. In the eastern tradition eating together signified a deeper shared fellowship. The customary Jewish supper, or *Chabura,* was a daily repetition of breaking bread and passing around the 'cup of thanksgiving'—a decided contrast to the cultic rites of the mystery religions. It was, in fact, according to Emil Brunner 'the hallowing of everyday living'.[21] One can therefore sense the import of this, their last meal together—an import which Jesus fully sensed at the time and which they would realise later. Then link the meal with the Jewish Passover observance and with the crucifixion which was now very near. In Jesus' mind they all converged at the meal, where he spoke of his yet-to-be-fulfilled Passover (Luke 22:15, 16), his body offered up for them, the cup of the new covenant (Mark 14:22-25; Matthew 26:26-29).

There is no question in our minds as to the importance of this meal. It was a highly significant event which embodied the new community which Jesus called into being through his life, death and resurrection. It is an event which the Church ought to remember. But it is much more than that: it is an event through which the Church is continually called to the Lord's table—that is, to the beloved fellowship of those who claim reconciliation through the cross, and consider themselves part of Christ's body, and are prepared to risk themselves for one another.

We recognise that the great majority of Christian fellowships observe the Lord's supper as a sacrament and that this observance is a means of grace whenever the believer partakes as an act of faith in the crucified Christ and as an anticipation of his Kingdom. Salvationists are not anti-sacramental; they are simply non-sacramental.[22] In the early days of the Salvationist movement, the Lord's supper was administered, and Bramwell Booth reports that many of these occasions were accompanied by great spiritual blessing, strengthening, vow renewal and even conversions.[23] But practical problems emerged and theological misgivings developed.

The practical problems themselves were considerable. Leaders feared that the large number of unschooled and simple converts would misunderstand the spiritual meaning of the sacraments and come to find security in their mere observance. Many of the converts were former drunkards, and the lack of availability of unfermented grape juice was a sizeable obstacle. The congregations at the Army meetings were usually a rainbow assortment of many types—uniformed Salvationists, other Christian supporters, the curious and a wide range of pagans, some of them rowdy, a few drunk. What criteria were to be used to determine who in this group would be allowed to partake, and who was going to make that decision? There was also the question of administration. Because laymen with leadership ability were often elevated to officership rank and given appointments with little if any formal training, many officers were not equipped to administer sacraments. Furthermore, and perhaps more importantly, the Army commissioned women as officers very early on, and the idea of a woman administering the sacraments was unthinkable in Victorian England. Finally, it should also be noted that as the observance of the Lord's supper became less and less frequent in the Army, William Booth suggested that Salvationists take communion in the Established Church, but alas, only the few who had been previously confirmed in the church were accepted. This barring of brothers and sisters from the table was an affront to the evangelical faith—and probably the last straw for William Booth. The institutional churches' table was not big enough.

There had to be a bigger table. Booth found it outside the sacramental liturgy of existing churches: he found it in the everyday life of the common man. If the Incarnation unleashed God's presence into the whole of human life, and if the crucifixion poured out his saving love throughout all the world, then there is no place where the table of his fellowship cannot be spread, there can be no such thing as a table where any disciple is denied. From its beginning the Army took a firm stand on the gospel for the whosoever. This stand led to major efforts to remove cultural and ecclesiastical barriers to both evangelism and fellowship. Frankly, the churches' reluctance to admit poor converts to the sacrament violated this major theological conviction of the Salvationist movement. But the conviction stood, and the sacrament went, for it confined the gospel to the existing ecclesiastical boundaries. Hence, the first theological misgiving over the Lord's supper arose over the perception—based on actual experience with ecclesiastical provincialism—that the sacrament had become a private celebration of cultural Christianity, a barrier to inclusive fellowship, and therefore a contradiction of Jesus' clear teaching on the Kingdom's openness to persons of all conditions and social classes (Luke 4:18; 14:15-24).

The second theological misgiving over the Lord's supper arose out of the Salvationist's evangelical pragmatism. We have already discussed some major practical problems that seriously discouraged the observance of this sacrament. Booth was impatient with any practice that stood in the way of the Army's evangelical mission to the masses. He had little use for methods or observances which, in fact, did not facilitate it. Not only were there practical obstacles to observance within the Army, the Church itself was seriously divided in its interpretation of what the sacrament actually was or what actually happened when it was administered, and in its discipline regarding admission to the table. In short, the Lord's supper was a source of continuing division within the Church. Should the movement, and especially its converts, be subjected to so much confusion over the observance of a ritual feast? Booth, the evangelical pragmatist, said no.

Third, there was in the movement a growing distrust of rituals as means of grace. We have already alluded to the anti-materialism of Catherine Booth and George Scott Railton.[24] If there was excessive disparagement of the physical in these passionate ascetics, there was also a needed prophetic voice against feasts, solemn assemblies and offerings which could bewitch Christians into a false sense of divine approval and could dull commitment to justice and righteousness (Amos 5:21-24). There is an ever-present danger to ritual observance, and the Lord's supper is no exception. The ritual can itself become a substitute for that which it is intended to assist in evoking. The participant in the Lord's supper can mistake the communion table for the real table and his imbibing for the reception of our Lord's grace through faith. The ritual for the real.

Yet the Army did not intend to eliminate rituals from the life of the fellowship. It has its own rituals and no less than any other must guard against empty ritualism. The abandonment of the Lord's supper had more to do with a fourth concern which, in our view, is the major theological rationale for Salvationist discontinuance.[25] We refer to the growing emphasis upon the call to holiness as the imperative for Christian character and lifestyle. As the movement became a 'church', that is to say, the church home for its swelling ranks of converts, greater attention was given to guiding these converts down the path of the new Christian way of life, which for many of them was a radical departure from their former ways. This necessity brought the movement's distinctive Wesleyan roots into greater prominence. Whereas the doctrine of salvation had been and continued to be the theological hallmark of Salvationism, the doctrine of holiness and the work of grace called sanctification were given increased attention as the key to the realisation of what God purposed for humanity through Christ's saving work.

We have seen that the holy life is the sacramental life, that sanctification is God's work of grace by which all of life becomes sacred and therefore every moment is a potential sacrament. If God is at the centre of every situation, if the Christian life is a pilgrimage in discovering and responding to his gracious presence in human life—a process which can also be described as growth in holiness—then sacramental rites are seen in a very different light. They are seen, not as prescribed occasions which have been designated as essential means by which God's grace in Christ must be experienced, but rather as celebrations of a far greater grace—the grace which is given to the whole of life and which consequently makes living a continuing sacrament. As a ritual observed in Christian worship, the Lord's supper is only a representation and reminder of the new sacramental life and the new community of fellowship in the Spirit which are made possible through Jesus' death and resurrection. It always points the Church beyond the celebration, to the living out of what the body broken and blood spilled made possible: the recovery of holiness of life and the restoration of fellowship with God and man. It is doubtful that the Salvationist movement would have discontinued the Lord's supper had this interpretation been that of the Victorian churches.

Perhaps it is not quite accurate to say that the Army 'discontinued' the Lord's supper. Let us say, rather, that the sacrament was transported from the high altar to the lowly meal table. It was taken out of the sanctuary and placed back into society. Could we be so bold as to say that the meal was brought closer to its origins in the early Church?

Listen to how the Acts of the Apostles describes the earliest sacramental meals of the Church in Jerusalem:

> And day by day, attending the temple together and breaking bread in their homes, they partook of food with glad and generous hearts, praising God and having favour with all the people (Acts 2:46, 47).

These and other such meals in the early Church were sacramental in the truest sense because, in their observance, the everyday became a remembrance of Christ's sacrifice (1 Corinthians 11:23-26) as well as a celebration of unity and mutual concern in Christ; the experience of this oneness led to honest self-examination of each participant's personal life in light of the new reality (11:27, 28), to confession of sin, to the experience of forgiveness, and to greater understanding of each other; and the remembrance of Christ's death and resurrection stirred the anticipation of his return (11:26). But they were basically common meals which became uncommon experiences because they were understood as an ongoing fellowship in Christ, a joyous celebration of his gift of himself, an expectation of the Kingdom's full realisation.

At first they were probably celebrated daily, especially in view of the expectation of Jesus' imminent return. However, as the Church spread well beyond Jerusalem, infiltrated the large urban centres of the Roman empire, broadened its national and cultural constituency and developed large congregations, the practicality of these 'love feasts' (as they came to be called) was lessened. There was no room for such big suppers! Furthermore, thoughts of dividing the congregation into groups for smaller, less supervised celebrations of the feast probably evoked both fear of the abuses which had sometimes plagued congregations previously and concerns about the possibility of factions emerging (1 Corinthians 11:17ff; Jude 12). Increasingly it seems, the love feast became associated with Sunday worship, which had established itself (as compared to worship on the Jewish Sabbath, Saturday) by the end of the apostolic period. At the same time, the more ritualistic aspects became prominent, and the Lord's supper gradually acquired the title 'eucharist' (meaning 'thanksgiving' and referring to the thanksgiving given over the bread and wine, the act which had become the primary 'ritual' of the supper). By the middle of the second century, the eucharist and the love feast were distinguished from one another, if not always separated.[26] The New Testament texts, however, document no such separation of rite from shared meal. We affirm, therefore, that the earliest remembrances and celebrations of the Lord's supper were as love feasts and that these observances were a part of the everyday life of the fellowship. They were not formal rites celebrated by separated priests; they were common meals which were transformed into transcendent experiences because the resurrected Christ was present at the table through the Spirit.

Vernard Eller writes that:

> the separating of the eucharist from the love feast was not the sloughing off of a minor element but a ripping of the ordinance right down the middle. Undoubtedly the only reason it could happen at all was that the service already had lost most of its original interpretation.[27]

He disparages prevalent interpretations of the supper which centre on the highly private act of incorporating the 'substance' of Jesus into oneself. Apart from the fact that such views deal in notions of 'being' and 'substance' which are foreign to the Bible, of greater alarm is the serious loss, or at least diminution, of the importance of the Lord's supper as a community event, as thanksgiving for the new covenant which binds the fellowship together, as a call to be broken for one another.[28] The popularity of the love feast among some religious groups in the 19th century, after centuries of neglect, may be attributable to a deep urge to repossess the communal dimension. The Moravians regularly observe the love feast, and some Methodist denominations have a distinct order of service for it. In the early days of the Salvationist movement, the love feast was observed in addition to the Lord's supper. When the sacrament was discontinued, the feast remained. However, its frequency has declined over the years. An article on conducting love feasts in the corps (Salvation Army congregations) which appeared in *The Officer* magazine in 1923, lamented that they 'seem to have dropped out of general use amongst us'. What is being lost, says the author (unnamed), is 'a means of promoting the spirit of love and unity, healing breaches and bringing about reconciliation between individuals or groups of persons in the corps. . . .'[29] The concern was clearly communal.

This brings us to the second major reality of the Church's life: life together. How does the Church celebrate and nurture reconciliation with God and man in the power of the Holy Spirit? Many sacramental churches observe the Lord's supper in such a way as to emphasise the unity of the fellowship through Christ's reconciling death and the call to give their lives for one another as Christ gave his life for them. Sacramental and nonsacramental churches alike can also observe the love feast as a less ritualised version of the early Christian common meal and approach it as an invitation to affirm the reconciliation of life in Christ by opening themselves to one another and accepting the responsibility of nurturing unity in Christ and service to one another.

The Salvation Army has retained a place for the love feast as a stimulus to reconciliation within the fellowship. The intimate atmosphere of a fellowship meal is created by a simple drink and bread or a plain biscuit. There are no *prescribed* elements: the drink can be water, grape juice, orange juice, tea, coffee, or something else, and the bread or biscuit can be of any kind. If it is possible, the chairs are usually arranged in a semicircle or a circle. The food and drink are shared from a common table by the corps officer(s) (pastor), sometimes assisted by local officers (lay leaders),[30] the words of Scripture are read, and a statement is made to the effect that this is not a sacrament but a fellowship meal, a celebration of oneness in Christ made possible by his death and resurrection. Reference is usually made to the last supper event as the prototype of the new fellowship and as a reminder that just as our Lord presided over that table in the flesh, even so he now presides over this table in the Spirit. It is in this context that the participants are invited to consider their own relationships. As thanksgiving is offered to God for the gift of reconciliation, opportunity is given for all to examine their interactions with other persons and ask whether they reflect the peace that has come in Christ. Then the leader challenges them to work on those relationships where enmity or apathy has had its grip, where healing is needed, and where forgiveness should be sought or extended. Sometimes reconciliations take place between members of the fellowship at the conclusion of the feast. The love feast is a celebration which has tremendous potential for encouraging the people of God to move decisively toward the defeat of enmity and the triumph of love in all relationships.[31]

Salvationist theology, however, moves beyond the *ceremonial* love feast. The love feasts which are conducted in the corps setting are really symbolic of what all meals are for those who invite the Christ to preside at every table. Bramwell Booth used to argue with regard to the faith through which the believer experiences grace in the sacrament: 'I see no reason why that same faith should not turn every meal into a sacramental feast.'[32] J. H. Jowett is faithful to this theology when he declares, 'That day is marked with glory when our daily bread becomes a sacrament.' Hence, the love feast cannot by its very nature be confined to ceremonial observance in an ecclesiastical setting. It is also a feast held day after day in the home and in the world. The *family* love feast is the celebration at every meal of Christ's reconciling presence in the home. The *spontaneous* love feast is the testimony of shared cups of coffee or meals outside the home as events which God in Christ wants to transform into a celebration—and realisation—of the peace that has come in Christ. In Salvationist understanding every meal partaken in fellowship with others is an invitation to share Christ and partake of his love. In all these settings the participants see the potential for Christ's reconciling work, and they fellowship as a witness and commitment to that work.

Bramwell Booth recalled some visits to an elderly man early in his ministry. In looking back he recognised that the humble meals with which these visits concluded were love feasts in the deepest sense. The man was a converted drunkard called 'Old Cornish' who had little of value, whose wife had died, he felt, largely because of his own former cruelty, and who was now a common costermonger. When Booth would visit to give spiritual counsel and pray, Old Cornish would prepare a sacramental meal of tea, fried bacon and potatoes. Booth writes:

> It was a veritable sacrament. When we knelt down together and when he began to pray he was so uplifted that it often seemed to me that he was another man. . . . And there came to me, in answer to those prayers . . . a new feeling of relationship to the souls of men, a new directional impulse, impelling me to love and suffer for the sake of others. Again and again I have come down those old squeaking stairs feeling as though I walked on the wind, and have gone out to Mile End Waste to speak and pray with sinners in altogether a new and self-forgetting fashion.[33]

Here was a fulfilment of our Lord's promise that where two or three were gathered in his name, there he would be in the midst of them (Matthew 18:20). Here Christ was presiding. Here, the Spirit transforming. Here, the love feast.

On many occasions prayer meetings have become love feasts in the Spirit. The Church is never closer to the Kingdom than when it is at prayer. Salvationist experience has borne this out. Intense sessions of prayer have frequently transformed a corps and led to revitalised mission. After visiting a Clapton Training Garrison prayer meeting, Dr Benson, Bishop of Truro, later Archbishop of Canterbury, remarked to Bramwell Booth, 'O, my dear brother, the Holy Spirit is with you!'[34] The Church at prayer is the Church reconciled, seeking the realisation of their life together in the power of the Spirit. They pray together in order to be together, to care together, to hope together, to travel together, to serve together. The prayer meeting is a sacramental celebration of the new community in Christ. It is the Church on its knees together before God, receiving the Kingdom anew, pledging service for its realisation, interceding for its enlargement in specific situations. It is the people of God getting down to the business of allowing the Spirit to empower them to live reconciled lives and to be agents of reconciliation in the world. Every true prayer meeting begins with a vision of the Kingdom and a prayer for its realisation ('Thy Kingdom come'), and ends with the body of believers presenting themselves as a living sacrifice to the God who can work redemptively to advance the Kingdom through those who will allow themselves to be broken for one another and for the world (Romans 12:1ff). Here also, the love feast.

How, finally, does the Church celebrate and nurture the third major reality of its life: servanthood? We must first point out that life for others ought to be implicit in both the sacrament of the Lord's supper and the celebration of the love feast. The reminder of Christ's body broken for us translates us into the new reality in which we are privileged to be broken for one another. We see in his broken body both the miracle which brings reconciliation and the principle for living reconciled lives. The representation of the new community in Christ which remembrance of the last supper evokes, also speaks powerfully of servanthood. Here, it is John's gospel that furnishes the most startling recollection:

> Jesus, knowing that the Father had given all things into his hands, and that he had come from God and was going to God, rose from supper, laid aside his garments, and girded himself with a towel. Then he poured water into a basin, and began to wash the disciples' feet, and to wipe them with the towel with which he was girded. . . .
>
> When he had washed their feet, and taken his garments, and resumed his place, he said to them, 'Do you know what I have done to you? You call me Teacher and Lord; and you are right, for so I am. If I then, your Lord and Teacher, have washed your feet, you also ought to wash one another's feet. For I have given you an example, that you also should do as I have done to you. Truly, truly, I say to you, a servant is not greater than his master; nor is he who is sent greater than he who sent him. If you know these things, blessed are you if you do them (John 13:3-5, 12-17).

Very few Christian denominations practice footwashing as a regular observance.[35] Yet Jesus' stated expectation that the disciples do likewise is very clear here ('. . . you also should do as I have done to you') as compared with the Synoptic gospels' accounts of the last supper, which give no indication of the institution of an observance or rite.

We do not argue that Jesus intended to institute the practice of ritual footwashing. Footwashing was a procedure in first-century Palestine made necessary by the wearing of sandals on dusty roads. A good host provided this hospitable amenity to his guests. While the guests reclined at table, a servant, or sometimes the wife of the host, performed the task.[36] Jesus' surprising assumption of this menial service was a parable more powerful than the spoken word. His action was so overwhelming that the disciples did not know at first what to do with it: Peter said, 'You shall never wash my feet' (verse 8). They were seeing an embodiment of the reason for Christ's coming, spoken before in words, now in action, soon in a crucifixion: 'For the Son of man also came not to be served but to serve, and to give his life as a ransom for many' (Mark 10:45). He who was in the form of God took upon himself the form of a servant (Philippians 2:5ff). In Jesus, almighty God approached us as our servant. No wonder the disciples were dumbfounded! They were witnessing the new Kingdom concentrated in a single action. As Jesus knelt before them with basin and towel, they were seeing divine humility born out of love willing to go to any length to save, they were unavoidably confronted with their calling to love and serve one another as Jesus did them, and they were being furnished with an illustration of cleansing from sin's defilement that was soon to be realised. Then Peter, on whom all this was probably beginning to dawn, exclaimed: 'Lord, not my feet only but also my hands and my head!' (John 13:9).

Jesus was giving us what may be his most significant parable of the Kingdom. As such, it is on a par with his last supper as a crucial event for the Church to remember and appropriate. Unlike the Lord's supper, the footwashing custom has no literal parallel in modern life. We share meals daily; but our feet are washed by ourselves privately. Hence, a symbolic footwashing would not have the psychological correspondence to contemporary intimate social life that the Lord's supper and the love feast do. But we wonder if an occasional symbolic footwashing among the gathered believers might provide a poignant reminder of who their Lord really is (Servant), what he went about doing (serving others) and what he calls them to (service of others). There is something about kneeling before a brother or sister in Christ and washing his/her feet that brings to the surface feelings of tenderness, appreciation for the sheer beauty of service of others, and awareness of the eternal significance of such a simple, mundane ministry. There is also something about having one's feet washed by a kneeling brother or sister that makes one feel that he is deeply honoured and appreciated as an important member of the family of God. If a footwashing ceremony can evoke such intimations of the Kingdom, if it can serve as a poignant reminder of our servant status and our calling to servanthood, then it may have value as a parabolic reminder of the new life in Christ which is not of this world, but given by the Spirit.[37]

A closing note about servanthood. We shall see in chapter 4 that the Church is called to be a servant in the world. This servanthood is based and built upon the mutual care and service that take place within the fellowship of believers. Washing one another's feet is a symbol of how Christians are nurtured into the fulfilment of their calling in the world. It is much more than a celebration of love at home. It is an equipping for loving the world for whom Christ died. When there is genuine, unselfish caring for one another in the fellowship, there is a constant overflow into the world in mission. The washing of our brother's or sister's feet is an act that points beyond itself, to someone lying wounded alongside a distant road, waiting for God's good Samaritan. We shall see that the same community which the Holy Spirit empowers to live redemptively is the community which the Spirit leads into a much larger world which cries out for redemption.

3

Called to a journey

The pilgrim people

The Church is a band of pilgrims who are called to separate themselves from the oppressive patterns of the present world order and to keep moving toward the possibilities which the new Kingdom in Christ offers.

PILGRIMS are literally people who journey, often in foreign lands. The image of the Church as a band of pilgrims embodies three key aspects of the Church's life in the world. First, it defines the Church as a people on the move. Second, it articulates the tentativeness of the Church's relationship to the social structures and behavioural patterns of contemporary society. And third, it suggests a Church which is moving toward the future—ie, to the destination of its pilgrimage. This third aspect will be the focus of chapter 6. In the present chapter we shall concentrate on the first two.

In chapter 2 we spoke of the sacramental life of the Church lived every day and everywhere. At first glance our talk of the Church's tentativeness and mobility in the world appears contradictory to this affirmation of God's redemptive presence in the common life. When we take a closer look, however, the contradiction disappears.

The Church in the world

As the new humanity and the redemptive fellowship, the Church is free to live its life *in* the world. As the object of God's love (John 3:16), the world is where the Church is called to live redemptively, give witness to the gospel and carry out its mission (Mark 16:15; Matthew 28:19, 20; Luke 24:47; Acts 1:8). Hence, the Church cannot exist in isolation from the world and remain the people of God. A church out of touch with the world is a church out of touch with God, for the call of God to go into the world is unmistakable. It was said of Jesus, 'He was in the world' (John 1:10). It must also be said of his disciples.

This is not to say that the Church is to conform to the patterns of the world or to compromise the gospel in any way. Nor is it to suggest that it take its orders from current trends and gives in to worldly faddism. It is to say that the Church takes its stand alongside the Word who 'became flesh and dwelt among us' (John 1:14). The incarnational basis of the gospel cannot be denied. God in Christ entered human existence, redeemed us in the world and made sanctification possible. In Christ the common becomes holy, and through the power of the Spirit the Church is called to holy living in the world. It is God's intention that his people live in the world as transformed people who seek the transformation of life in all aspects. The Church is called into the world to celebrate God's redemptive presence in the common life and to be a transforming fellowship through which he can demonstrate the power of God unto salvation.

In our view, the image of the Church as the pilgrim people of God sheds light on the way this calling is realised. Because pilgrims are on a journey, they are not tied to the structures and *status quos* of the society in which their pilgrimage takes place. Always on the move, they value flexibility and tend not to invest their lives in structures that stifle spiritual creativity. They are always becoming.

Now, how does this view reconcile with our understanding of the Church as the redemptive fellowship which celebrates the sacramental character of everyday life? The answer is that God's graceful presence in human life is best discerned and experienced by those who are on the move in their own spiritual development. Those, on the other hand, who are tied to blind dogma, perfunctory ritual, and institutional self-preservation, those who see God as guardian of the *status quo* (no matter how oppressive it may be), have so institutionalised God in their thinking and feeling that they are unable to see him at work outside their narrow—and usually self-serving—perceptions. Pilgrims, however, have the view of a wider horizon, they are open to new experiences of God; to them, everyday life can reveal God's presence in extraordinary ways. They see God around them because they are not in captivity to their environment.

One of the most potent and useful metaphors of the Church's involvement in the world without acquiescence to destructive, spirit-killing entanglements, is the biblical view of the people of God as *a nomadic people on the move.* Consider the wandering Hebrew nomadic tribes of the Old Testament. Consider the rootless folk who made up the majority of the early Church. Consider the significance of this statement by the writer of the letter to the Hebrews:

> For here we have no permanent home, but we are seekers after the city which is to come (Hebrews 13:14, *NEB*).

It may be that Christianity's truest appeal is to rootless people! They are the least tied down to the static structures and the stubborn *status quos* of this world. They are freer to move ahead. They are more open to new possibilities for the future. Hence, their views of life tend to be more dynamic, and they more easily accept the present order as temporal.[38]

Another biblical metaphor which captures both the mobility of the pilgrim Church and its focus on the world, is that of the *military.* The implications of this metaphor for the Church will be explored in greater depth in chapter 4. Suffice it to say for our purposes here that the concept of the soldier at war is a fitting analogy of the Christian who is committed to mission in the world and whose whole life is wrapped up in that mission. In the words of George Webber it

> . . . expresses the character of [the Christian's] life. In Christ men enter into his warfare. . . . No civilian role is possible. Even off the military reservation the professional soldier is on duty, in uniform, unlike the peacetime man who performs military duty on the army base and then dons civilian clothes off the post.[39]

The people who are willing to adopt this radical, militant pattern of life are those who are open to change, those who are willing to leave the familiar behind, those who are willing to sacrifice security for participation in God's redemptive, but painful, mission in the world. They truly seek another Kingdom and because of their commitment to that Kingdom and its realisation in human life and history, they do not allow themselves to become entrenched and entangled in the reactionary sectors of the world order which resist the Kingdom.

Eller uses the interesting analogy of a *caravan* to describe the pilgrim life of the Church. Described at first as 'the Way' (Acts 9:2; 18:25; 19:23; 22:4; 24:14, 22), the New Testament Church drew from the Old Testament understanding of God as leader-lord who beckoned his people to move beyond the enslavement of their present state, as in the Passover and the Exodus. In this context:

> . . . salvation cannot be understood as a state of having it made, of settling down to enjoy a condition of secure accomplishment. Salvation is the experience of being made free to travel, of being called out by a leader-lord and enabled to follow him on the way that he is making toward the kingdom.[40]

Eller goes on to contrast the caravan Church with the commissary Church. The former sees itself as a fellowship of pilgrims who are always on the way in response to their Lord who goes before. They place more stock in progress than in ritual. They value the contribution of each member of the caravan. The latter, on the other hand, sees itself primarily as an institution that dispenses goods, services and benefits to a particular constituency. Emphasis is therefore placed on the position of the one who does the dispensing (the minister or priest), as well as the importance of following correct procedures in doing so.[41]

It is our conviction that the analogies of the caravan in motion, the people in pilgrimage and the army on duty best describe the New Testament understanding of the Church as in the world but not of it. Those who are overly invested in the world and consequently tied down to its order find it difficult to pull up stakes and discover the freedom to move beyond their culturally conditioned understanding of life and living. Those, on the other hand, who are travellers with God have an unlimited horizon, a rewarding journey and untold excitement before them.

Jesus himself gave ample warning of over-investment in the world. For example, he pointed out the great difficulty which a rich person would have in entering the Kingdom (Mark 10:25; and parallels, Matthew 19:24; Luke 18:25). He told a parable which derided the rich man who invested in bigger and better barns in order to build his personal security and indulge in his wealth (Luke 12:16-21). His answer to the query of the Jewish leader who wanted to know how to receive eternal life and who had kept all the commandments, was that the man needed to sell his possessions and give the money to the poor (Luke 18:18-22).

Jesus was not, of course, glorifying poverty and condemning wealth wholesale. There is nothing inherently blessed about the sordidness and squalor of most poverty; nor does wealth necessarily corrupt. What *is* the case is that worldly entanglements of any kind impede one's pilgrimage—even family obligations, for example, can stand in the way of discipleship (see Luke 9:59-62)—and personal wealth easily becomes an entanglement.

We should point out, however, that the poor *also* can become entangled in consuming hope for a reversal of the economic order, or they can become entangled in their fear and despair. One's social or economic condition in life does not automatically determine one's relationship to the Kingdom. What is important is commitment to a life which does not consist in what a person *possesses*—or does *not* possess (see Luke 12:15).

The pilgrim lifestyle

We have come, then, to a further development of our ecclesiology. We have come to see the Church as God's pilgrim people who are able to fulfil God's purpose for them in the world because they are not paralysed by investments in the oppressive patterns and entanglements of the present world order. They are a people who are free to move as the Spirit leads.

Now, how do we see this reality at work in the life of the Church? What characteristics of its faith and practice embody its calling as a pilgrim people?

Let us look, first, at the doctrine of *sanctification.* Sanctification, as we have seen, is the gracious act of God by which the sacramental life (holiness) becomes possible. It infuses all of life with a vision of divine possibilities; the sanctified Church looks for God at all times and aims to live in continual response to his presence. This ever-present search for the revelation of God in every situation and this bias toward patterning life accordingly, are characteristic of a pilgrim people. As those who are on a lifelong journey, the Church is a people who possess nothing, and therefore have everything. As the company of those who have left security behind to follow their leader-lord, they receive a hundredfold in this life, and in the life to come (Mark 10:28-30). As those who seek first his Kingdom and righteousness, they find that other gifts of life are theirs as well (Matthew 6:33).

Those, on the other hand, who are bent on possessing this world, or a part of it, fight a futile battle. 'The earth is the Lord's, and the fullness thereof . . .' (Psalm 24:1, *AV*). It is the setting for pilgrimage, not self-aggrandisement. It is a place for temporary tents, not towering temples. The world belongs to those who know to whom it belongs. It belongs to those who have been adopted into the family of the Owner: those for whom the 'world' is now seen as the always unfolding terrain of God's self-revelation. It belongs to those who have no interest in possessing it and are therefore the only ones who have it. It belongs to the meek (Matthew 5:5).

The meek are those without presumption. Consequently they are suited for pilgrimage. Seeing little for which to commend themselves in their present estate, they live in readiness to keep moving on to something better. They are the travelling Church which is open to God's leading and influence. They are the sanctified.

We see, therefore, that the life of holiness is the appropriate description of the character of life of God's pilgrim people, the Church. How, then, can we describe the *lifestyle*? It has two key characteristics. The first is a willingness to risk, and the second is discipline.

Pilgrims are people who take risks. Any journey involves an element of risk. The traveller accepts this reality, not because he finds danger to be pleasurable, but because his destination, or the purpose of the trip, is worth the risk. God's people are those who risk pilgrimage because it is the only way for them to see what God wants them to see and become what God wants them to become.

More than once in the Old Testament, the Israelites had to be reminded that they were a pilgrim people who could follow their Lord's leading only through a willingness to risk. When Moses was ready to lead them into Canaan, he sent out spies, one from each of the twelve tribes, to gather intelligence. When they returned only two of them, Caleb and Joshua, recommended entry; the rest cautioned against going against a foe that was 'stronger than we' (Numbers 13:30ff; 14:1ff). Clearly the majority were not ready for entry, and entry was not made at that time. Instead, there was delay and further defeat.

This 'grasshopper mentality' (see Numbers 13:33) is a disease that attacks the Church's calling as God's pilgrim people. The apostle Paul reminds his more timid spiritual son, Timothy, that the fear to carry out his calling does not come from God. Rather, from God comes 'a spirit of power and love and self-control' (2 Timothy 1:7). As those who follow the leading of their Lord, the Church is the company of those who must journey and must consequently accept the risk of facing the unknown and undergoing personal change. Religions of safety have no place here.

The second characteristic of the pilgrim lifestyle is discipline. We are not referring to repressive discipline, nor to discipline for discipline's sake. These are the tools of a society that seeks conformity rather than change. What we have in mind is the kind of discipline without which there can be no real progress, the discipline of one who keeps himself in condition for spiritual travel, the discipline which steels God's people for the challenges. It is the laying aside of every impediment to pilgrimage and of the clinging sin which ties us to the oppressions of the present world order (Hebrews 12:1) so that the spiritual journey can be made.

Without such discipline worthwhile risks will never be taken; the fear of new spiritual ventures will never be overcome. It is no coincidence that Paul names 'self-control' as one of the antidotes to Timothy's spirit of fear (2 Timothy 1:7). Only the disciplined can direct their efforts and maximise their strength sufficiently to overcome obstacles, endure hardship and do the risky things that pilgrims must. The undisciplined, on the other hand, are forever open to attack; they are easily defeated; and so they live in constant fear. Theirs is not the lifestyle of pilgrims. God's pilgrim people are people of courage who have been nurtured by discipline.

Ministry and tradition in the pilgrim Church

Let us move on from here to an understanding of ministry which the interpretation of the Church as a pilgrim people requires. If holiness describes the life, and courage and discipline the lifestyle, how can we best describe the ministry?

The pilgrim calling of the Church implies an understanding of ministry which is both dynamic and democratic—dynamic because the pilgrim Church is always on the move, and democratic because each pilgrim has something important to contribute to the forward movement of the caravan.

A *dynamic* understanding of ministry emphasises the prophetic over the priestly, function over status, mission over maintenance. A Church on the move has more need for leaders who will discern and speak the word of God than for those who will maintain the traditions. It has no time to create an ecclesiastical hierarchy; ministry must be seen in a functional way as the exercise of Spirit-given gifts for building up the body of Christ (1 Corinthians 12:4ff)—that is, for enabling the Church to move forward in its pilgrimage. It has a strong bias toward carrying out its divinely mandated mission in the world (1 Peter 2:9), and this missionary disposition overrides the ever-present pressure to put down roots and opt for a settled existence. If the pilgrim Church lives in a terrain which is constantly changing, and if it is always in the process of becoming, then all its ministry is dynamic service toward the destination of its spiritual pilgrimage.

A *democratic* understanding of ministry centres on the calling and contribution of each pilgrim. Not only is the New Testament clear that all Christians have a calling and election (see 1 Peter 2:9 again), it is also clear that all callings are equally important (Romans 12:3ff; 1 Corinthians 12:20ff) and that Christians in secular occupations are to pursue these as callings of Christ (Ephesians, chapters 5 and 6). The Church in pilgrimage needs the service of all who travel, and the mission of the Church in the world can be carried out effectively only through the exercise of the various gifts given to the fellowship of believers.

The doctrine of the priesthood of all believers, therefore, has a profound affinity to the view of the Church as God's pilgrim people. Privileged priests tend to be a function of static, hierarchical religious institutions. Ministry shared by all and apportioned according to recognised gifts bestowed by the Spirit, tends to be a function of a dynamic community of faith which is ever on the move.

From this perspective of a pilgrim Church engaged in a dynamic shared ministry, how are ecclesiastical *traditions* to be viewed? It could be said that the Church exists in the tension between inheritance and pilgrimage, between what the people of God take with them on their pilgrimage and what they leave behind, between the practices of yesterday and the challenges of the new situation to which these forms may no longer be relevant.

Since the true Church is always on pilgrimage, the problem arises in distinguishing between that part of its tradition which is essential to its integrity as the people of God and that part which is temporal and needs to be altered or replaced in the face of the requirements of a new phase of the pilgrimage. One tradition is discarded at the peril of the Church losing its gospel, the other is discarded for the advantage of paving the way for the development of ways suitable for the new phase of the Church's pilgrimage. A tension is created because it is often difficult to distinguish clearly between the two and because outmoded traditions often survive past their time by becoming sacralised and institutionalised.

One helpful way to see the tension is to use the analogy of a plant. If we compare Church tradition to a plant, then we can say that the roots are more important than the branches. Without the roots there is no plant. Not only do the roots stabilise the plant, they are also the primary means of nourishment. The branches can be pruned—and doing so often makes for a healthier plant—but the roots must remain basically intact. We must seek to understand what are roots and what are branches in Church tradition. We must know what can be discarded (pruned) and what must remain. We must also understand the conditions under which pruning is appropriate.

One condition is when the branches become too overgrown and cumbersome. Tradition can become a proliferation of life-sapping branches weighting down the plant and preventing purposeful growth. Christians can become so bogged down in proliferated church activity and ritual that they lose sight of and fail to receive adequate nourishment from their spiritual roots. When this happens, the only healthy course of action is the pruning of tradition—that is, the elimination of extraneous practices that no longer serve the essential purposes of the Church—so that new, and more purposeful, growth becomes possible. A particular practice, for example, which developed under certain conditions as the most appropriate way to achieve an essential objective of the Church in a given situation, may or may not still be the best means to the desired end. In some cases it may have become so irrelevant in the present situation as to stand in the way of achieving that objective! Sometimes the mere continuation of the practice gives the illusion of progress toward the goal, when in fact regress is the reality.

Hence, when it comes to Church tradition we can see where two dissimilar analogies correspond: a people on the move must shed extraneous baggage and a healthy plant must shed useless branches. Pilgrims must continually decide what to take and what to leave behind, and those decisions must be based upon the destination of the pilgrimage and the nature of the terrain. In the same manner, the Church as God's pilgrim people is always in the process of reshaping its life so as to be prepared for each phase of the journey and responsive to the leading of its Lord. For them, faithfulness to tradition is not adherence to traditions; it is adherence to the gospel, allegiance to Christ, openness to the Spirit's leading—and letting the chips of tradition fall where they will. Sometimes the chips will fall right into place; there are traditions worth continuing, at least for the time being. Other times the chips will fall by the wayside; most traditions eventually outlive their evangelical usefulness. In order to fulfil its calling as God's pilgrim people, the Church must courageously maintain flexibility in matters traditional. While never belittling the forms inherited from the past, it must not hold them fast at the risk of leaving the commandment of God (Mark 7:8). At all costs and with every necessary adjustment, the journey must be made.

Celebrating and nurturing the pilgrim calling

Having described the key characteristics of the faith and practice of the pilgrim Church, let us now consider the ways in which the Church celebrates and nurtures those characteristics.

First, let us consider *the celebration of the pilgrimage begun.* Traditionally this celebration has been marked in the rite of baptism. Baptism in the Church has its roots in the baptism of converts to Judaism, a practice which came into being after the close of the Old Testament period. The rite signified the transition from pagan life to membership in the community of Israel. It was not only a religious rite of passage but also the symbolic representation of the beginning of a new journey. As a sign of repentance and turning one's life in a new direction, Christian baptism marked the beginning of the pilgrim way. In its early form, carried out in the open wherever there was a body of water, would-be pilgrims were initiated for journey in the very settings in which they lived their lives. Later on, when the Church and its worship had become institutionalised and baptism was moved into the sanctuary, it began to lose its emphasis upon the initiation of a pilgrimage and moved instead toward the conferring of a status. Furthermore, the increasing practice of infant baptism reinforced the endowment character of the rite.

While recognising that saving grace is a gift of God through Jesus Christ and that any adequate celebration of conversion to Christ must convey the reality of this undeserved endowment, a Salvationist ecclesiology also insists that celebration must adequately represent the truth that saving grace makes pilgrimage possible. To stop short of conveying that a journey has now *begun* is to miss the very purpose of Christ's saving work. He came to make us disciples who grow like him by travelling with him. Whatever the rite by which conversion is celebrated, it must represent this new beginning.

In chapter 1 we spoke of two public acts in Salvationist practice that give witness to response to the call to discipleship. One is kneeling at the mercy seat and the other is enrolment as a soldier. Actually, the two are of a piece with one another: the enrolment represents the outcome of conversion. What begins with the penitent on his knees concludes with the new disciple on his feet, standing under the flag that represents his new life in Christ.[42] Here the new soldier reaffirms his vow to follow Christ and joins the company of pilgrims. Those who are present for this occasion are invited to renew vows, and together they may sing this verse of Salvationist songwriter Doris N. Rendell:

Saints of old obeyed the call;
At thy word they gave up all;
Where they trod so valiantly,
May we follow fearlessly.

Mighty Captain of the host,
Fill us with the Holy Ghost;
Suffer not our feet to stray
From this new and living way.

(*The Song Book of The Salvation Army*, No 789, verses 5, 6)

Much of Salvationist hymnody is journey-oriented. It borrows the pilgrim music of an amended John Bunyan hymn:

He who would valiant be
    'Gainst all disaster,
Let him in constancy
    Follow the Master!
There's no discouragement
Shall make him once relent
His first avowed intent
    To be a pilgrim.

(*The Song Book of The Salvation Army*, No 685, verse 1)

But it also contains numerous songs by Salvationist writers which capture the intense joy of those who travel the pilgrim pathway. These words of Charles Coller are almost euphoric:

Make the world with music ring,
While with heart and voice we sing
Praises to our God and King,
  Hallelujah!
Tell with no uncertain sound,
To the nations all around,
Of the Saviour we have found,
  Hallelujah!

(*The Song Book of The Salvation Army*, No 809, verse 1)

Unable to understand the rapturous celebrations of early Salvationists, Thomas Huxley sought to dismiss the phenomenon with his coined phrase 'corybantic Christianity'. But what he was seeing—without perceiving—was the sheer joy of people who had been going nowhere, and now were travelling to a God-given destination. Salvationist singing, clapping and witnessing are spontaneous expressions of a Church in pilgrimage.

Let us now move to a consideration of *celebrating the pilgrimage sustained.* Many congregations celebrate the Lord's supper in such a way as to call attention not only to Christ's sacrifice and his redemptive presence through the Holy Spirit, but also to his leadership and Lordship in the Church's ongoing pilgrimage in the world.[43] In this context the bread and wine are also understood as representations of the nurture for pilgrimage which is given through the Christ who is present and the congregation which is his Body.

A Salvationist ecclesiology, however, sees the love feast as a more apt celebration of the pilgrim life of God's people. As a more spontaneous and less institutionalised rite, it is better suited to the journey. Salvationists committed to the sacramental life seek God's presence in every situation, and especially where life is shared at the deepest levels. No place more fittingly symbolises this sharing than the meal table. For those who are in Christ, any meal can become a love feast when his presence is shared. It was in the breaking of bread and the sharing of fellowship at a common meal that two despondent men travelling to Emmaus recognised the presence of their resurrected Lord—and not before (Luke 24:13-32). This was a love feast because the presence of the Lord of love was recognised. And any meal is a love feast where he is present in fellowship. The pilgrim of God needs no priest to present the elements and mediate the Presence; the elements are at every meal, and the Presence is God's gift made available at every occasion of shared fellowship.

The love feast, then, is a celebration of Christ's presence with and leadership of his pilgrim Church in every part of the journey. In it he reminds his people that they are called to a pilgrimage which requires sacramental living and mutual caring. The sacrifice of Christ for the world becomes the model for Christian sacrifice, and Christ's ministry of nurture and support becomes the model for a like ministry inside and outside the Christian fellowship. This meaning of love feast is perhaps best summed up in these words of Albert Orsborn:

> My life must be Christ's broken bread,
> My love his outpoured wine,
> A cup o'erfilled, a table spread
> Beneath his name and sign,
> That other souls, refreshed and fed,
> May share his life through mine.
>
> (*The Song Book of The Salvation Army,* No 512, verse 1)

If the love feast, then, is a poignant reminder of Christ's redemptive presence with his Church and the shared life of the fellowship as the realities that sustain the Church in its pilgrimage, by what means do the people of God nurture and celebrate *the pilgrimage equipped*? Our understanding of ministry as dynamic and democratic derives from a pilgrim understanding of the Church in which gifts for ministry are given for the facilitating of the Church's pilgrimage and its mission in the world. The Church requires a view of ministry which is dynamic because it is carried out in a changing terrain, and democratic because every pilgrim on the journey has a vital role to play in nurturing the Church's forward movement.

These key characteristics of ministry in the pilgrim Church are celebrated primarily through *ordination.* We see disparity between New Testament accounts of initiation for specific ministries—Jesus sending out the Twelve (Matthew 10:1-5), the appointment of the seven for clear-cut tasks of service (Acts 6:1-6), the commissioning of Barnabas and Saul (Acts 13:1-3), for example—and the subsequent development and domination of an understanding of ordination which focused on a status conferred in the initiation rite. By the Middle Ages, there were three major orders (bishop, priest and deacon) and four minor (acolyte, exorcist, lector and doorkeeper). Outside these orders there was no ordination to ministry. The Protestant Reformation recovered the democratic understanding of ministry in its doctrine of the priesthood of all believers. However, its practice, as well as its theology, has not always kept faith with the doctrine. Protestants have also succumbed, from time to time, to the unbiblical view that ministry is for a spiritually privileged class only.

The understanding of ordination which arises out of a Salvationist ecclesiology can be described in the word *commissioning.* It suggests that someone is being formally assigned to carry out a specific responsibility or go on a special mission. This emphasis on function or mission, rather than ecclesiastical status, broadens the concept of ministry to include everyone in the fellowship. All pilgrims have a role to play in the travelling Church. Each is commissioned for ministry according to his spiritual gifts, talents, resources and personal readiness. It is important to note that the term 'commissioning' also connotes a communal dimension to what is taking place. A Latin word from which it is derived refers to an act of bringing together. Commissioning for ministry, therefore, implies—and even requires—that there is a coming together in community, a common mind and heart about what is being undertaken, a sharing of resources, the inclusion of all members of the fellowship in support. There is no ministry in isolation.

In Salvation Army practice, soldiers are commissioned to specific responsibilities. This is true of both laymen and ministers. Officers are ministers who have undergone vocational training for the ministry, culminating in two intensive years of study at an officers' training college. Local officers are laymen who pursue other vocations as well as serve in specific capacities in the corps (local congregation). Both are commissioned to a ministry.

Clearly, there are 'status' overtones to the Army's military form of ecclesiastical government, and there have been those who mistakenly viewed the officership calling as spiritually superior to that of the local officer. Furthermore, the Army has its share of dormant laymen and is sometimes myopic in its view of spiritual gifts which do not 'fit' traditional understandings of the organisation's character and mission. As true as all this is, however, there are principles behind the commissioning concept which are atuned to the New Testament understanding of calling to ministry: that all God's people are called to specific ministries, that the Church is charged to give spiritual direction in discerning and developing individual gifts for ministry, and that each member is to be commissioned to carry out responsibilities which best utilise his gifts.

No Salvationist ecclesiology is adequate which does not affirm this inclusive calling to ministry because it is based on both scriptural imperative and Salvationist heritage. It was a part of the genius of the early Salvationist movement that it invited one and all to join the caravan of pilgrims and to play a needed role. Common working men were given the dignity of rank and responsibility. Women, to whom most avenues of leadership and service were closed in the 19th century, were challenged to match their gifts with their calling, and large numbers became officers and local officers—much to the chagrin of most Church leaders of the day. Hence, the rite of commissioning is an intentional celebration of the call to ministry addressed to *all* pilgrims in a Church which is on the move and in need of the exercise of all gifts.

It also embodies the dynamic understanding of ministry because of its emphasis on mission rather than maintenance. Commissioning for ministry implies that there is a task to be done, progress to be made, a battle to be fought. It suits the pilgrim Church, which places little stock in the *status quo* and great stock in forward movement under its Lord's leadership. It is a celebration of God equipping his pilgrim Church for the journey.

We conclude with the question of Church structure and government. If God equips his Church for a ministry which is both dynamic and democratic, how is that ministry to be structured? What is the form of government for a pilgrim Church? How does the Church pattern its life in a way that expresses and facilitates its pilgrim calling?

We agree with the view that the New Testament sanctions no particular form of ecclesiastical government—episcopal, presbyterian, or congregational. Rather, in each setting the Church seems to have ordered itself in accord with principles of government which correspond to the social and cultural setting and to the requirements of its mission.[44] As the creation of the Holy Spirit and as the pilgrim people of God, the true Church orders its life in ways that encourage redemptive living and foster forward movement under its Lord's leadership. Authentic Church government allows both space and direction for spiritual development, encourages the growth of fellowship in the Spirit, adapts itself to meet the practical requirements of new phases of the Church's pilgrimage, and (as we shall see in chapter 4) facilitates the Church's mission in the world.

No one form of ecclesiastical organisation insures these benefits. Furthermore, we recognise that each particular form tends to be biased toward certain strengths and susceptible to particular abuses. After a democratic approach failed to provide the avenues for needed charismatic leadership and daily decision making in a rapidly expanding movement, The Salvation Army opted for an episcopal form of government expressed in the language of the military. (Since the Army was involved in missionary work which brought open attack and required mobility, the military metaphor suggested itself quite naturally.) This form of government has served the peculiar calling of the Army well. It has fostered decisive leadership, courage in times of trial, mobility, adaptability, focus of action and clear-cut goals. It has also encouraged lay participation: membership meant being a part of an Army at war; there was a role for every soldier to play.

But there are inherent weaknesses in this, as well as in every form of ecclesiastical government. When the battle wanes, or becomes more diversified, it is much more difficult effectively to involve all soldiers. Gradually, leadership tends to be monopolised by a hierarchy of professional officers. Institutionalisation brings greater preoccupation with the army itself and often diminishes the priority of the battlefield.

How can The Salvation Army, as well as any other denomination, withstand the insidious pull toward rigid hierarchy and immobile bureaucracy? The final three chapters of this book will address this concern in various ways. But at this point we can return to the focus of the present chapter and assert that one of the important keys is for the Army to live and govern itself as a pilgrim people. A Church in pilgrimage will have shared ministry and responsive leadership. Regardless of the form of government, decision making and structure will be suited to the journey.

A Salvationist ecclesiology, therefore, does not posit one form of church government as superior to others. Any form is useful that furthers the pilgrimage. In practice such a form actually becomes a tangible *celebration of the pilgrimage actuated.* It celebrates the pilgrimage because it facilitates the journey. It helps the Church to separate itself from the oppressive patterns of the present world order and to keep moving toward the possibilities which the new Kingdom in Christ offers.

In conclusion let us point out that the nature of the Church as a pilgrim people corresponds to the nature of the Christian life. The Christian is a pilgrim who is called to move from death to life, from darkness to light, from slavery to freedom, from sin to forgiveness, from enmity to peace, from hatred to love. But this journey, while personal in the deepest sense, was never meant to be a private undertaking. Whether he knows it or not, every Christian is part both of the one host of God's pilgrims through all ages and of a particular band which nurtures him in his contemporary journey. The writer of Hebrews is addressing a *band* of pilgrims when he writes:

> Therefore, since we are surrounded by so great a cloud of witnesses [the host of pilgrims through all ages], let us [our present band] also lay aside every weight, and sin which clings so closely, and let us run with perseverance the race that is set before us, looking to Jesus the pioneer and perfecter of our faith . . . (Hebrews 12:1, 2).

The Church is comprised, then, of bands of pilgrims who are called to move together from life which is captive to sin, to life which is captained by Christ and liberated by the Spirit; to move together from meaningless patterns of living, to spiritual vitality; to move together from the kingdoms of this world to the Kingdom of their Lord and of his Christ.

What is so important is that the Church *keeps* moving. From first to last, the Church is in pilgrimage. Its calling is in danger when it stops. But when it moves, there is hope that the way will be found.

4

Commissioned for battle

The army of salvation

The Church is an army which exists for the purpose of fighting every enslavement to sin, disarming the causes of human oppression, and overcoming obstacles to pilgrimage.

AS we have seen (chapter 3), the concept of the soldier at war can be effectively related to the view of Christian living as pilgrimage. Likewise, the Church as an army to the Church as a pilgrim people. A Church on the move is a Church at war. As we shall see, the two descriptions are inseparable. In order to understand the military application, we must state the purpose of the Church. In other words, the characterisation of the Church as an army derives from the reason for which it exists in the world. What is that reason?

The purpose of the Church

The reason is *mission.* The Church exists primarily for the sake of its mission in the world. Because of this essentially missionary nature and calling, the focus of its life and structure is the world for whom Christ died. This purpose is carried out, not by allying with the present world order, but by proclaiming and demonstrating the life of the Kingdom that has come in Jesus and by calling the world to this radically new order. In doing so, the Church becomes a pilgrim people who beckon the world to free itself from despair and make pilgrimage toward God's hopeful future. But in doing so it faces the opposition of those forces which impede the progress of the Kingdom in human life. There is no way to avoid this opposition without compromising the Church's mission. The battle must be joined. The Church is an army.

But how can this be? Are we abandoning our previous assertion that the Church is a fellowship of believers-in-the-peace who know peace with God, themselves and their neighbours (chapter 2)? If reconciliation has taken place in Christ, if the decisive battle is over, why is the Church an *army*?

We must understand, first of all, that living by the peace treaty does not bring avoidance of strife. Rather, by freeing itself from commitments to those behaviours and processes that oppose the treaty, the Church places itself outside of and over against the world order. The world order operates out of the assumption that the world is at war with itself and peace is merely an alliance which is temporarily advantageous or a stand-off which is temporarily needed. To repudiate this assumption is to bring opposition from the world which embraces it.

The champion of Christ's peace consequently finds himself at the centre of conflict. Only now the conflict takes a different form. Having prophetically witnessed to the peace of Christ and exposed the unreality of the state of war, he himself becomes the focus of antagonism from those who cling to the myth of a fragmented world. In this process the conflict is transformed: instead of being a conflict between parties who accept the same view of reality, it becomes a conflict between contradictory views, and those who pursue war now find that they must deal with those who are at peace. Since the reality by which the Christian lives exposes the unreality (ie, the ultimate meaninglessness and futility) of the pursuit of war and challenges persons to undergo profound change and abandon the ways of enmity, conflict often becomes focused on those who represent the peace.

The conflict is thereby transformed. It becomes redemptive. The prototype is Christ on the cross. The cross is the place where refusals to accept the peace which Christ offered were directed with deadly force. But at the same time, the cross is also the place of victory—the place of defeat for the principalities and powers of a warring world and the place of triumph for the reconciling Christ (see Colossians 2:15). In facing cruel death brought on by enmity and by his refusal to adopt the ways of enmity, he fully exposed enmity's ultimate powerlessness. His death, then, became the beginning of life, the way to resurrection, and as such signalled the end of death-dealing enmity. The Church in mission takes this reality seriously by challenging the validity of situations created by enmity, by helping to reshape them in the light of Christ's peace, and by suffering the consequences from those who refuse the peace.

To accept the peace of Christ, therefore, is not to turn one's back on a strife-filled world. Rather, it is to be empowered to reach out to the world with a caring heart and a willingness to pay a price for the peace. It is to be at peace and in love at the same time. It is to live by the peace and to invite others to live by it.

The Church, therefore, is a peace-keeping force in the world. But it is more. It keeps the peace in the sense that it seeks to live by the peace. But its position in the world is not neutral. It is not trying to maintain a cease-fire between other warring parties. Rather, it is a peace-keeping force in a world that opposes the peace and that consequently attacks the keepers of the peace; and it is a movement dedicated to inviting enemies to abandon enmity and accept peace. It is an army of the gospel of salvation-through-reconciling-love. It is a salvation army.

The Church in the New Testament, in fact, is militant in its posture. Never in a position of rest or final triumph, it is always either doing battle or preparing for battle. Harvey Cox has pointed out that the figure of the soldier was used more frequently than any other to describe the life of the Christian in the world.[45] According to Hans-Ruedi Weber, in New Testament times the decisive act of becoming a soldier in the Roman armies was called the *sacramentum,* or the military oath. The Church later adopted this same word to signify the decisive act of becoming a soldier of Christ. Baptism, and especially the vows taken at baptism, came to be called the *sacramentum.*[46] The Christian, in contrast to the 'pagan', saw himself as having vowed absolute obedience to Jesus Christ and as having committed himself to participation in Christ's battle for the world. The early Church, therefore, was something like an army, and its activities alternated between making camp in preparation for battle and breaking camp to do battle. Committed both to the reality of the Kingdom in Christ and to the battle for its realisation, Christians at peace fought battles for reconciliation.

Implications of the commission

This understanding of the Church as a missionary army carries important implications.

First, it means that *the Church cannot automatically identify itself with the world or with any particular culture or society.* For the sake of the integrity of its mission, it must maintain a critical distance. It must, as we have seen, be in the world but not of it. It must live a simple life so as to be free to focus on the essential issues and fight the worthwhile battles. It must live a disciplined life so as to maintain obedience to the Commander-in-Chief (Jesus Christ) and not allow itself to become entangled in civilian affairs that would jeopardise that obedience.

Second, the description of membership as soldiership means that *there is no room for passive membership.* In this sense, 'soldier' is a better word than 'member'. Members can be passive or active; they may do no more than belong on the rolls. Soldiers cannot only belong; they are either fighting or maintaining readiness for battle—otherwise, they are not really soldiers. To put it differently, the objectives of a society or club are usually primarily internal; the objectives of an army are primarily external. Hence, the Church's use of the military metaphor is symbolic of its external purpose: mission in the world.

Third, the view that the Church is in the world to do battle implies that *it must be both mobile and flexible.* The New Testament Church stood in readiness to follow the leading of its Lord. Following his leading often required new departures, different methods, structural changes, radical personal adjustments, shifts of emphasis, readiness to move on. No two battles are the same nor are they fought on the same battlefields. A Church which is called to do battle must be ready to move out to the new battlefield, to survey the new terrain and to adapt its fighting methods accordingly. A Church, on the other hand, which is committed to ritual battles on outdated battlefields and to the preservation of its own historical structures and methods for the sake of institutional survival, is a Church that has lost its capacity to do battle—and hence its missionary purpose. An inflexible and immobile Church is no Church at all; it is a religious relic.

Fourth, if missionary warfare is the focus of the Church's activity, *preparation for battle is the main concern of its internal life.* The military training camp, where soldiers receive support and are challenged to prepare for carrying on the battle, is a good model for the Church's internal life. It implies that mission is the dominant and controlling passion of the Church and that every aspect of the Church's life ought therefore to be seen as contributory to mission in one way or another. Activities such as worship, group Bible study, Sunday-school classes and membership (soldiership) training classes can be planned and implemented with a focus on mission. Even such activities as therapeutic groups, parent groups, sharing groups, problem-centred groups and the like can be seen as missionary in that they foster the health, well-being and personal growth of both persons being equipped for mission and persons reached in mission. In other words, they focus on aspects of human life which the new Kingdom in Christ transforms and thereby give witness before the world to the redemptive living which the Holy Spirit makes possible. Small groups in the Church are at the same time both battlefields and training camps: they are the settings in which persons struggle most decisively for healing, wholeness and community, and as such they stimulate the personal growth and renewal by which participants are prepared for carrying out the Church's mission in the world.[47]

Fifth, and lastly, since the Church is an army involved in war, *each member (soldier) must be prepared to lay his life on the line:* 'Share in suffering as a good soldier of Christ Jesus' (2 Timothy 2:3). There is no war without sacrifice, and where there is no sacrifice, no real war is being fought. A good soldier is obedient to his commander-in-chief. All other loyalties take second place to this one overriding allegiance; the *sacramentum* is absolute. The decisive test of the Church's seriousness about mission is the readiness to remain loyal to Jesus Christ when loyalty demands risk, loss, radical change and even death.

A Salvationist ecclesiology takes these implications of the Church's missionary calling seriously. It sees the Church as an army of salvation which has sworn allegiance to Jesus Christ as Commander-in-Chief and has been commissioned to do battle. Let us now address the matter of how this reality is at work in the life of the Church. How does the Church realise its missionary calling?

The answers to this question come under two broad areas. The first area is how the missionary Church organises for battle. The second is how it fights its battles.

How the missionary Church organises for battle: a structure that serves the mission

Since the Church exists for the sake of its mission in the

world, its life must be so ordered as to implement this priority. George Webber states that

> on every level and at every stage, order has a single purpose: to enable the church to deploy its forces most effectively in its assigned mission in and for the world.[48]

We have seen that ecclesiastical tradition exists in order to facilitate the Church's pilgrimage. When it impedes pilgrimage, then it must be altered or discarded. In the same way, its purpose is also to further the mission of the Church in the world, and it must be judged both by its faithfulness to the gospel and by its effectiveness in advancing mission.

Robert Paul proposes an ecclesiology based upon the principle of 'evangelical pragmatism', which insists that the Church must be free to meet the spiritual needs of every age. This ecclesiology:

> . . . recognises the claim that in the light of the Church's essential task all ecclesiastical institutions are secondary, if not irrelevant, and that if institutional structures are to be used from time to time, they should be set up to meet the needs of the moment and should be modified or discarded as soon as the immediate task of the Church has been fulfilled. When that task is clearly understood as the proclamation of 'the faith which was once for all delivered to the saints' (Jude 3), we are speaking about a kind of 'evangelical pragmatism'—a pragmatism that is brought into the service of the gospel.[49]

Paul discusses John Wesley as a classic proponent of this ecclesiology. At first Wesley was very suspicious when George Whitefield introduced him to open-air preaching, for he was concerned about decency and order in the Church. But a few days later, he '. . . submitted to be more vile, and proclaimed in the highways the glad tidings of salvation'.[50] The furtherance of the Church's mission required new methods. Hence, for Wesley:

> the nature of the Church was ultimately to be governed by the nature of the evangelical task given to God's people: this was its first and basic characteristic.[51]

Historically rooted in the soil of the Wesleyan revival, the Salvationist movement shared this same ecclesiological principle. A Salvationist ecclesiology, therefore, holds that everything connected with the ordering of the Church's life and work must serve its missionary calling.[52]

One important way to build structures that serve the Church's mission is to emphasise *process* rather than *form.* It is far more crucial to preserve the process that has shaped a missionary tradition than the forms which that process has created. At best, certain traditions came into existence as appropriate ways to facilitate the Church's mission in a particular context. They may, or may not, still serve that purpose effectively. If not, they should be altered or replaced by new forms when they no longer facilitate mission in the present context. The spiritual truth that death must come before life applies to institutions as well as to persons.

The ever-present danger to the integrity of the Church's missionary calling is the security—if we can think of security as a danger—of hiding behind practices and structures that no longer serve that calling. It comes when Christians are lulled into believing that the continuation of a tradition or method is synonymous with the implementation of missionary goals. The early Salvationist movement was positively brilliant and courageous at discarding forms which were irrelevant and adopting new ones that served the contemporary mission field well. But along with other denominations, it must today be willing to depart from many of the practices of its forebears in order to be faithful to what those forebears were doing in mission in their day—and most importantly, in order to be faithful to the God who *still* leads his Church in mission.

Another important way to insure that structure serves mission is for the Church to organise its whole life and work around its missionary purpose. We shall call this *missionary unity.* Here again we see the relevance of the military metaphor: an army tends to be united in a common purpose. John Wesley used the language of warfare when describing the Church's unity in mission:

> I desire to have a league offensive and defensive with every soldier of Christ. We have not only one faith, one hope, one Lord, but are directly engaged in one warfare. We are carrying the war into the devil's own quarters, who therefore summons all *his* hosts to war.[53]

In an address at Exeter Hall, London, on 'The Future of Missions, and the Mission of the Future', William Booth proposed the reorganisation of the Church into 'one vast missionary society' in which all Christians were committed to the scriptural prophecy of '. . . the time when the devil is to be vanquished, evil to be driven out of the world, war is to be at an end, and peace and righteousness are to overspread the earth'. All Christians, in other words, would be united in this common cause.[54] Early Salvationists, therefore, were urged not to become provincial in their thinking and not to become too absorbed in their local corps congregations. Rather, they were to keep in mind that they were part of a universal mission committed to the gospel for the whosoever. Sectarianism, therefore, was seen as a scourge on the missionary Church. It undermined the unity which was so necessary for the success of mission. Unlike the sectarians who placed great stock in their own peculiar doctrines and organisations, Catherine Booth insisted that

> . . . God cares very little about our sectarian differences and divisions. The great main thing is the love of God and the service of humanity. . . .[55]

It was not surprising, therefore, that the Army distilled its doctrinal statements to what its early leaders considered as the missionary essentials: eleven doctrines over which there was general agreement among Wesleyan evangelicals. Eliminated were minor and divisive points of doctrine which were the bases of much sectarian bickering and denominational polarising.[56] In doctrine as well as in organisation, missionary unity was the object.

There is yet another key task in building structures that serve mission. It is described in the word *adaptation*. The missionary Church maintains sufficient flexibility to adapt to the terrain in which it serves. In chapter 3 we described the Church as a pilgrim people on the move. This tentativeness in relation to the world encourages a flexibility which enables the Church to readjust itself for each new challenge in the changing terrain.

The process of adaptation assumes that God is at work in the constantly changing world and that much of that change is a manifestation of his activity, or at least of the possibilities for change which he is creating. If the Church's mission is to be responsive to God's activity in the world, then it must maintain an ability to take advantage of the opportunities which this activity offers. Such missionary flexibility focuses on the manifestation of God's presence and work rather than the survival of pre-existing missionary structures and assumptions. It thereby provides an openness to the world which facilitates creative mission in changing communities.

Hence, the missionary Church is flexible enough to follow its Lord into the new territories which he is opening up for mission. The 'new territory' may be in the form of: fresh opportunities for evangelism; a new socio-economic situation in which previous ways of ministering are no longer meaningful; a change in the racial or cultural character of the community calling for an adaptation of the ministry of the gospel to the new constituency; the opportunity and need for a specialised kind of ministry; the emerging struggle of a neighbourhood community to survive internal and external threats and develop its potential as an affirmative living environment; or any new situation through which God calls his people to pull up stakes, enter new missionary territory and fight new missionary battles. Response to this call will always entail breaking out of and moving beyond previous mission structures. It will also require a willingness to risk leaving familiar territory and entering new terrain. Every Christian missionary must learn to abandon what is no longer promising.

William Booth preached the principle of adaptation, and his Army was a demonstration of the principle in action. Insisting on the abandonment of any evangelistic method that was no longer effective, he called upon his soldiers to invent new methods; and these new methods became the distinctive features of a movement which risked the ridicule which departures from the *status quo* always bring. He hated the thought that this Salvation Army might one day become 'respectable'.

One of the most effective means of cultivating adaptability in the missionary Church is the small group. We shall describe small groups involved in mission as *mission teams.* Utilising teams in mission provides clear-cut advantages.

First, the mission team can be effectively used to *strengthen commitment to the universal gospel.* Small groups in a congregation can offer differing styles, focus on differing concerns, informality as compared to the greater formality of larger gatherings, greater allowance for addressing individual needs, and the choice of a smaller social setting within the congregation which more closely approximates the cultural setting from which a new person comes. This breadth of appeal through small groups geared to particular needs is a powerful weapon for use against social barriers which the Church has often allowed to impede its mission.

In addition to small groups designed to attract persons with specific needs, there are task-oriented missionary groups formed by members of the congregation to develop a community ministry. Such groups have definite capabilities for implementing an inclusive mission. In the first place, because of the typical informality and person-to-person character of small group relationships, the mission team is better able to move beyond the kinds of tacit assumptions and prejudices which often control congregational policy and action. Their missionary consciousness having been raised, they will be likely to become active in mission. In the second place, the team can pursue Bible study and prayer at a high level of intensity and in an atmosphere encouraging personal application. When such study and meditation focus on the Church's missionary calling, the cause of the universal gospel is bound to be strengthened. And in the third place, the mission team, because its primary purpose is mission, is likely to be more flexible and better able to meet new missionary challenges than a large congregation with diverse commitments.

Second, the mission team can effectively *implement the ministry of evangelism.* In the early Salvationist movement, soldiers were organised into 'brigades' for specific missionary tasks, and these groups became important vehicles for evangelism. There are four reasons why small groups can be so effective in evangelising. In the first place, they are highly adaptable. They can meet in a variety of settings outside the institutional church, at the convenience of the persons who are being reached. In the second place, they can organise themselves around specific tasks and determine their own format. For example, the task may be an ongoing informal discussion of the meaning of commitment to Jesus Christ. Two of the goals could be: (1) to empower Christians to witness and (2) to present the gospel to others who are attracted to the group. In the third place, small groups can provide a setting for honest searching. They can offer understanding and support for those who are struggling with faith, guidance for those who are asking questions and hope for those in despair. In doing so, they will lead some to faith. And in the fourth place, they can function as vehicles for training Christians to witness.[57]

Third, the mission team can *organise for battle.* Because modern Christian warfare must take place in a shifting, pluralistic terrain, it requires a 'guerilla style' which relies on the strategies of smaller commando units which are adaptable to the exigencies of the war. It also requires disciplined units which understand their military objectives and maintain combat readiness. The mission team is ideally suited for this disciplined pursuit of objectives and the adaptation of structure and method to the needs of the battlefield.

In structuring for mission, therefore, the Church organises its life in ways that facilitate the flexibility and mobility required for combat readiness. In order for such an organisation to fulfil its purpose, it must be comprised of mission teams, or other manageable units, which implement clear missionary objectives. We now turn to the question of how missionary warfare is conducted.

How the missionary Church fights its battles: evangelism and social action

The mission of the Church is based on the gospel. The gospel is the good news announcement of the new situation in Jesus Christ, the Kingdom which is now reality because of his life, death and resurrection. The mission of the Church, therefore, is to participate in that reality and give witness to it. What the Church does in mission is based on the potential for pointing to the saving presence of Christ in the world, to the reality of the Kingdom of God's love, to the reconciliation which has taken place through the healing power of Christ's death and resurrection.

The Church gives witness to the gospel primarily in two ways. These can be described as *evangelism* and *social action.* Both are concerned with facilitating the transformations which the reality of the Kingdom makes possible. Evangelism is concerned with transformation on the personal level, and social action on the socio-economic level. Evangelism is an announcement of the Kingdom's presence and an invitation to accept citizen status. Social action is also an announcement of the Kingdom's presence, but in this case by supporting and participating in the social change for which that presence calls. Without both ways to witness, the proclamation of the gospel is hindered. Evangelism without social action is flight from the world and refusal to accept the reality of the Kingdom's transforming presence in the midst of this world which God loves.[58] Social action without evangelism is flight from the personal depth of the gospel and refusal to take seriously Jesus' unmistakable command to his followers to become 'fishers of men' (Mark 1:17; Matthew 4:19; Luke 5:10).[59]

People used to suggest to William Booth, 'You know, General, we can do with your social operations, but we can't do with your religion; we don't want it.' The General would reply,

'If you want my social work, you have got to have my religion; they are joined together like the Siamese twins, to divide them is to slay them.'[60] For the Church in mission, evangelism and social action go hand in hand. Otherwise, the gospel is perverted. In reality, one cannot hear the message of the Kingdom without personally confronting the one in whom it is present, and one cannot receive the Kingdom without confronting its implications for the world into which it has come and still comes.

If, then, evangelism and social action describe the two ways in which the Church fights its missionary battles—the two *kinds* of Christian warfare, if we please—and if the war, in order to be engaged, requires both, then what is the *weapon* with which it fights? The answer is given by Jesus: 'Love your enemies . . .' (Matthew 5:44; Luke 6:27). The statement itself is an intentional contradiction. By definition, enemies are hated. Christians, however, are those who live by the peace that has come in Christ and therefore have no enemies. But those who would be enemies do not know this; they do not know, or are afraid to know, that they are not enemies. The only way to show them the reality of reconciliation in Christ is to love them, to treat them as friends and to do so at a cost. Missionary warfare is really love-fare, and the weapon is love because love is the un-weapon. Evangelism and social action, therefore, are the twofold expression of a Church in love with the world for whom Jesus died and at war with every attitude, assumption, force and law which contradict the Kingdom.

It should be clearly understood, however, that evangelism and social action are more than the ways in which the Church carries out its mission in the world. They are also expressions of what is taking place within the fellowship of believers-in-the-peace. They are not merely charitable acts toward those who are outside the fellowship. Rather, they are the 'overflow' of Christian caring within that fellowship. Members of the Christian family need to hear the gospel again and again, and in all its implications, and given the opportunity continually to be renewed and transformed by it. They must be given the space to repent and grow. They must be freed to minister to one another. They must be empowered to change ecclesiastical processes and structures that alienate persons and stifle missionary vitality. When this nurturing and growth take place within the fellowship, there is an overflow which occurs, and the overflow is the mission of the Church. The mission is the external expression and sharing of what is happening internally. Otherwise it is merely charitable works on behalf of outsiders. Evangelism and social action are the refreshing and renewing overflow of the life of the Church. In carrying out its mission, the Church is actually embodying not so much what it thinks it should *do*, but what it *is*.

The missionary Church, then, is nothing other than the Church following its Lord, leading its sacramental life, travelling on its pilgrim way—and inviting others to do the same. Only as such is it an army of salvation commissioned for battle. Only as such is it engaged in warfare. For the Church at war, there is no human enemy. In fact, persons are seen only as potential recruits. The enemy is sin in all its personal and social forms—all of which seek to destroy the God-given integrity of human life. As long as this battle for the human soul rages, the Church will be commissioned for battle.

How the Church celebrates its missionary purpose and nurtures its missionary preparedness

A Salvationist ecclesiology places major emphasis upon the means by which the Church cultivates its missionary character and strengthens battle preparedness. Let us consider these means under three major headings: battle commissions, battle support and training, and battle organisation.

There are specific rites in the Church which rightfully ought to stress the Church's missionary calling and charge the Christian undergoing that rite with his/her missionary responsibility. We hold that such rites ought to have the character of, or culminate in, the issuance of a *battle commission.*

We have already described the relationship between the *sacramentum*, or military oath, and the rite of baptism in the early Church. In adult baptism the believer was not only immersed for the remission of sins, but he vowed absolute obedience to Jesus Christ as his Commander-in-Chief. Whatever ordered to do, he would do; wherever sent, he would go. Baptism meant that he was commissioned for battle. We hold that all adult baptisms practised today are authentic expressions of New Testament faith only if they charge the new believer to become involved in the Church's mission in the world as an integral part of his Christian discipleship.

When enrolled as a soldier, the new Salvationist not only

affirms his salvation in Christ, his responsibility as a member of the body of Christ, and his embarkment on a new pilgrimage, but he also vows to be a missionary soldier:

> . . . I do hereby declare my full determination, by God's help, to be a true soldier of the Army till I die. . . . I do here and now, and forever, renounce the world with all its sinful pleasures, companionships, treasures and objects, and declare my full determination boldly to show myself a soldier of Jesus Christ in all places and companies, no matter what I may have to suffer, do, or lose, by so doing.
> . . . I do here declare that I will spend all the time, strength, money and influence I can in supporting and carrying on this war. . . .
>
> And I do here and now call upon all present to witness that I enter into this undertaking, and sign these articles of war of my own free will, feeling that the love of Christ, who died to save me, requires of me this devotion of my life to his service for the salvation of the whole world, and therefore wish now to be enrolled as a soldier of The Salvation Army.[61]

These words from the articles of war, which are signed by all Salvationists who are enrolled as soldiers, leave no doubt about a battle commission. Neither does the ceremonial commissioning of local officers: (lay leaders). Even the Salvationist marriage ceremony includes the furtherance of the Salvationist mission as an important goal of the marriage!

We hold that ordination to the (full-time) ministry ought also to emphasise a commissioning for battle. We have raised serious questions about interpretations of ordination that stress the conferring of a unique spiritual status. Rather, we hold that all Christians are called to ministry and mission and that full-time ministry, while exceptional in some ways, is not essentially different from lay ministries. The difference is in the combination of gifts required, the extensive development of professional skills for ministry undertaken, and the time for formal ministry committed. Ordination, then, is commissioning to specific ministries within the context of the Church's mission—ministries that require theological training, specialised skills, pastoral leadership and a full-time vocation. Placed within this missionary context, the ordained ministry can only be understood as functional—that is, through the exercise of gifts for ministry, as serving the purposes of the Church's mission. The rite of ordination ought to convey that function and celebrate the missionary purposes which are served by it.

We have seen, then, that the missionary Church commissions

all its members for battle. Now let us ask how it provides *battle support and training.* Earlier in this chapter, we discussed the importance of the Church's unity in mission. If, in fact, the Church exists for the sake of its mission in the world, then every programme should contribute toward the implementation of that mission. Early on in his ministry, William Booth became deeply concerned about both the short-lived effect of many independent evangelistic campaigns and the churches' lack of missionary focus and commitment. Consequently, his Salvation Army came into being as a movement united in its missionary objective and organised to carry out its mission. He formulated a 'doctrine of combination' which stressed the work of the Holy Spirit in uniting believers to carry out this mission.[62] In his view, every programme of the Church ought to be a part of the total support system for mission.

Many of the Army's departures from traditional Church practices and rituals are best understood as missionary enhancement by addition, subtraction and alteration. Military terminology was adopted as an effective way to underscore and foster the missionary purpose of the movement. It helped to maintain the atmosphere of battle and the commitment to mission. Salvationist songwriters wrote of the spiritual warfare in which the Army was engaged and urged their comrades to remain faithful on the field, confident that their Lord would be victorious. Even as recently as 1946, Will Brand would write:

Earthly kingdoms rise and fall,
    Kings and nations come and go,
Thou, O God, art over all,
    None thine empire shall o'erthrow.
Of thy grace are we enrolled
    In the train of thy dear Son,
Pledged our faith undimmed to hold
    Until victory is won.

High o'er rampart, tower and wall,
    Faith her standard proudly flies;
Youth obeys her trumpet call,
    Marching forth to grand emprise.
In each hand uplifted high
    Gleams a consecrated sword;
Hark! they shout their battle cry:
    Rise and fight for Christ, our Lord.

(*The Song Book of The Salvation Army,* No 799, verses 1, 2)

This kind of enterprise required numerous changes for the support of missionary warfare among the working-classes. Static ecclesiastical symbols, for example, were replaced by mobile symbols; symbols of mediation were replaced by symbols of mission. The Army adopted language, practices and customs which represented departures from the established churches and made the Christian faith more available to the working man. The clear intent was to remove the gospel from the prejudice and confinement of sanctuaries which were foreign to his culture. It was to reject the assumption that the experience of God was confined within the walls of churches for the privileged. It was to bring an awareness of God redemptively at work in the world and outside the institutional Church. It was to move Christianity to a new missionary front.

Hence, in the place of the Lord's supper administered in sanctuaries was the practice of every common meal as sacramental. In place of the high altar was the freedom to kneel and pray anywhere. In place of the procession to the altar was the march in the streets. In place of the stationary symbolisms adorning sanctuaries and worship services were the mobile colour symbols of blood (redemption) and fire (sanctification) on uniforms and flags.

Further support for missionary warfare was provided by the expectation of a simple and disciplined lifestyle. It did not take William Booth long to see that the Salvationist mission would require this kind of lifestyle on the part of its soldiers and officers. By the time the movement formally adopted the name The Salvation Army in 1878, it had evolved by natural process into a disciplined 'army'. Soldiers were expected to commit their talents, time, effort and money to the mission war and to shun involvements that would detract from this commitment. They were to avoid certain harmful indulgences (eg, alcohol and other drugs) and maintain high ethical standards. Their lifestyle was to support the integrity and effectiveness of the mission.

Another support for missionary battle is the love feast. This statement may at first sound strange, but not when we remember that mission warfare is love-fare. In this context the love feast is a celebration of the love of God in Christ Jesus as the power that both binds the fellowship together in the Spirit and unravels it for mission. In fact, the love feast reaches its full meaning only in fellowships committed to mission. The gospel does not allow for celebrants to affirm only the unity of the fellowship; it requires the support of mission as the overflow and outreach of Christian caring. The missionary love feast is a celebration of the love of God in Christ in its dual manifestation of the holy communion and missionary commission of the saints.

The Church takes seriously its commission to mission not only through celebration, language and other forms of communication and nurture, but also in developing concrete plans for training members for mission. It is a mission training centre. We have discussed the suitability of small groups for missionary training and action (the mission team). Small groups formed to implement specific missionary objectives are also learning and training centres. In addition to such groups, congregations may also offer other opportunities for mission training. Mission seminars may be conducted by the congregation, or interested members sent to other seminars or training workshops. Regular events can be scheduled that allow for such training. For example, the traditional 'soldiers' meeting' of Salvation Army corps can be effectively utilised in this way. The important point is that the congregation intentionally plan and implement a mission training programme. Without such a programme, there is no missionary credibility.

Finally, let us consider the Church's *battle organisation.* How can the Church and her local congregations so organise themselves as to maximise missionary preparedness and effectiveness? In chapter 3 we saw that a Salvationist ecclesiology does not posit one form of church government as superior to others. Rather, each form of government is to be judged in relation to its effectiveness in facilitating the Church's pilgrimage in that particular setting. Now we must add to this requirement: not only must church government facilitate pilgrimage, it must also further mission. The Church must be organised for battle.

Let us now evaluate the government of The Salvation Army in relation to its effectiveness in furthering mission. We do this as a case study in mission government, not in order to claim any superiority of Salvationist government.

Whereas Salvationist government is episcopal in substance—that is, authority resides in a 'bishop' rather than in the local congregation or a judicatory—William Booth said that he had found more practical help from the regulations of the British Army than from the disciplines and methods of the churches.[63] It is our view that the primary reason for the evolution of the military *modus operandi* was the missionary focus of the movement. Militancy signified universal mission. During the time when the change in name from The Christian Mission to The Salvation Army was being finalised, Booth announced: 'The Christian Mission . . . has organised a salvation army to carry the blood of Christ and the fire of the Holy Spirit into every corner of the world.'[64] The change to a military form of government did not take place overnight but rather evolved naturally as an effective form of mission government in the milieu of the late 19th century. What were the reasons for this effectiveness?

First, a military approach to its mission and its methods enabled the movement continually to be reminded that because the Kingdom had not yet come in its fullness, there were still many battles to be fought. The Salvationist had to live in a state of readiness and preparation for battle. All the numerous spiritual, social and political battles in which the Army was involved were seen as part of God's ongoing warfare of love in the world. Salvationists were committed to fight until the Kingdom dawned in its full splendour. There was no resting until that day. The Church was called to be the missionary army of God.

Second, the military form of government encouraged the simple and disciplined lifestyle necessary for mission. In chapter 2 we discussed simplicity of life as characteristic of the redemptive fellowship. It is also characteristic of the Church at war, the Church disciplined for battle. As is the pilgrim, the fighting soldier is also a stranger in the land, and if he becomes too settled, he loses his ability effectively to do battle in that terrain. He must maintain missionary discipline and singular commitment to missionary purpose. The military lifestyle seemed to William Booth to be the best mode for this discipline and commitment, and in fact the Salvationist movement had already evolved by natural process into a disciplined 'army' by the time the name The Salvation Army was adopted. The military pattern provided a very useful *modus operandi* for the discipline required of a missionary movement.

Third, the military organisation created an environment and a system that encouraged lay participation. Studies have shown that, on the whole, the only kind of church membership available to the poorer classes of Victorian England was membership in name only.[65] Booth knew that a missionary movement designed to reach the poor would succeed only if it offered them full participation in its life and mission. Hence, by design, his movement took on the character of a volunteer army which all were invited to join and in which every participant was given an assignment. One of the early songs began with 'Come, join our Army, to battle we go. . . .' 'There's a place for every warrior . . .' went the line of a popular chorus. As the army at war engages its soldiers, so the Church in mission employs its members.

Fourth, the movement's military organisation provided a capacity for mobility which its missionary purpose and the international scope of that purpose required. As an army the movement was able to spread around the world like wildfire. During the 1880s it grew from an organisation confined to the British Isles to an international army fighting in most of the major areas of the globe. The major contribution to this phenomenal missionary expansion made by the military form of government cannot be gainsaid.

The Army's autocratic government was itself a very significant factor in increasing mobility. The correlation of autocracy and mobility may at first seem strange, but not when the subject is an army at war. Many situations on the missionary battlefield require a powerful leader who can act decisively. The early Army was a rapidly expanding international movement which required effective continuity of purpose and method and an efficient, expeditious decision-making process. Government by committee proved woefully inadequate. The constant need to respond to missionary challenges required leadership which could effectively mobilise the movement. By popular choice William Booth emerged as that leader. The decade following this governmental change was marked by extraordinary growth, rapid international expansion and the beginning of serious involvement in social reform. It culminated in the publication of Booth's comprehensive social scheme for dealing with poverty and economic depression in Great Britain, *In Darkest England and the Way Out.* The student of Salvation Army history could hardly fail to acknowledge that these missionary advances would not have been possible without a strong central government.[66]

Fifth, the movement's military organisation fostered adaptability to the missionary terrain. An important key to the Army's ability to make inroads among the working classes in industrialised countries and indigenous cultures in non-industrialised countries was its understanding of itself as an army fighting the forces of Satan wherever he tried to claim territory in God's world. In order to do so, it had to live off the land, understand its inhabitants and adapt to the terrain; and by doing so, it became a truly international mission.[67]

Examples of the principle of missionary adaptation in the early Army are numerous. We will cite only a few. At the beginning we should point out that the entire movement evolved as a church for the poor and working classes, first in England and then in other countries as well, and that it consequently adapted its language, rituals and methods to the understanding and character of that culture.

One of the most important strategies for adaptation was the movement from chapel to street. William Booth discovered that most of the poor would not enter chapels, but *would* listen on the street corners, where they frequently congregated. He therefore re-emphasised the open-air service which John Wesley had utilised in the previous century. This strategy carried certain risks. Ruffians frequently attacked the street corner evangelists, and early on the municipal police often tried to deal with these disturbances by putting the Salvationists in jail. But persecution usually strengthens a movement and attracts new followers. The Salvationists endured the jeers, egg throwing, physical violence and incarcerations. It won them the support of the poor.

Another important strategy for adaptation was the adoption of language and means of expression which were native to the working class culture. Since the formal hymns of the Church had little appeal to the tastes of the unchurched poor, Booth encouraged the use of popular tunes, even those associated with drinking songs, as settings to religious words:

> You must sing good tunes. Let it be a good tune to begin with. I don't care whether you call it secular or sacred. I rather enjoy robbing the devil of his good tunes. . . .[68]

He also adapted the religious language of the Church to the understanding of the common man. In his first systematic book of doctrinal and organisational instruction for The Salvation Army he wrote:

> When talking about the forgiveness of sins is it wise to avoid such terms as regeneration, justification, and the like?
>
> Yes. Because the common people, indeed, people generally, do not understand what is meant by them. Use the plain words, pardon and conversion. Everybody will then know what you mean.[69]

As the movement spread around the world, it attempted to adapt to the culture of the poorer classes everywhere. Babu Keshab Chandar Sen, leader of the Brahmo Samaj in India, had said that India would accept Christ when he took off his hat and trousers and boots. Not long after the Army commenced its work in India, *The Indian Mirror* of Calcutta declared:

> If The Salvation Army can prove that Christianity is really the religion of the poor; that it can doff lavender-coloured breeches and . . . patent helmets to put on the mendicant's ochre garb; that it can dance, shout and march with the ordinary proletarian poor human nature from the mill, the mine and the workshop; if The Salvation Army can prove that, it will have done enough service towards the future evangelisation of India.[70]

Records of the Army's early work in India substantiate that significant inroads were made in successfully adapting to the culture of poorer castes. Progress was concrete enough to cause the Governor of Bombay, Sir James Ferguson, to fear in 1882 that the newly arrived Salvationists '. . . might break down the barriers between Europeans and Indians and lower the prestige of the white man'.[71]

Salvationist adaptation to the cultural and socio-economic condition of the particular classes it sought to reach in mission was not the only form of adaptation it practised. It also adapted itself to the exigencies of the war. For example, excess baggage which did not serve mission goals was often left off. This was particularly true in matters of theological formulation. Complex doctrines were simplified, and many of the doctrines that were the foci of acrid theological disputes were eliminated. The battlefield was no place to squabble over differences in theology. Booth reduced the articles of confession to what he considered to be the basic essentials. As far back as the early days of The Christian Mission—the name by which the movement was known before it became The Salvation Army—it had been decided that no one would be disqualified from membership because of 'minor questions of doctrine' so long as such differences did not detract from the prime function of the Mission.[72]

The essential doctrines, therefore, were those that were directly supportive of mission. Wesley had simplified the Thirty-Nine Articles of the Anglican Church to twenty-five for the American Methodist societies. Booth simplified to a bare eleven doctrines. Ignoring the metaphysics of doctrine, he retained only those he considered necessary for faith, and therefore for mission. As far as the eleven doctrines themselves were concerned, he usually refused to be drawn into disputes over differing interpretation. For example, while asserting the necessity of belief in the inspiration of Scriptures, he made no detailed argument for any particular theory of inspiration. In the missionary Church, doctrine gives focus and unity, not diversion and division.

We have tried to show that the Army's military form of government fostered missionary effectiveness. It nurtured a state of readiness and preparation for battle, a simple and disciplined lifestyle, lay participation, mobility and flexibility, and adaptability to the missionary terrain. But we must also raise some critical questions. The Army's use of the military pattern has facilitated its missionary faithfulness in the past, but at the same time it has created certain limitations and even dangers which need to be recognised and addressed.

First, it should be recognised that the use of a military pattern and form of organisation, and the symbolic use of military language, do not necessarily mean that worthwhile missionary battles are being joined. They may mean only that the rituals of a tradition are being perpetuated. Furthermore, the military pattern does not ensure any capacity to adapt or mobilise for new battles on new terrain. An army can easily become immobile and inflexible, and incapable of meeting new battle challenges.

Second, the autocratic form of government needs to be evaluated in relation to the contemporary mission field. In the early days of the movement, an autocratic government provided efficient decision-making, responsiveness to the field and international cohesion. Today, a complex and top-heavy bureaucracy encourages autocratic decision-making which is slow, cumbersome and insufficiently responsive to the needs of the field. Autocracy needs to be mediated by grassroots participation in planning so that it retains its relevance to the mission field.

Third, uniformity of procedure and method needs to be evaluated in the light of an increasingly pluralistic milieu. Even the Army itself has become much less monolithic and more diversified in character. What needs to be recognised is that greater social and cultural pluralism within the Army expands the movement's capacity to minister in a highly pluralistic terrain. Organisational pluralism can increase missionary effectiveness by offering more options in method and providing appeal to a wider range of social groups.

Fourth, the Army's predilection for action as opposed to reflection needs reassessment. Armies, of course, are by nature action-oriented. Theirs is not to ask *why,* only to find the most effective means of achieving the received objective. Historically, The Salvation Army's strength has been the ability to respond quickly to missionary challenges. It has been scarce on theological tools with which critically to evaluate its responses. We have seen that in the early days doctrinal simplification served to reduce theological considerations to the basic essentials. One hundred years later, however, the Army is seriously in need of developing theological tools with which to be discriminating and responsible in its warfare. This is not a plea for spending more time on fine points of theology. It is a plea for the development of an ongoing theology of mission informed both by Scriptures and tradition and by the contemporary situation.

Fifth, care needs to be taken to avoid an idolatrous pitfall: the spiritualisation of the Army's regimented structure. Such spiritualisation would obscure the sociological realities which underlie its life and structure and consequently cause organisational blindness. A poor grasp of these realities within the fellowship produces a parallel ignorance of important social dimensions in the missionary terrain. Army structure needs to be looked at objectively in relation to the movement's stated missionary purpose, with a view to maximising the achievement of that purpose.

The above critique is given in the interest of a battle organisation which serves mission readiness and effectiveness. As an army of salvation, the Church exists for the purpose of overthrowing the enemies of God and freeing persons for pilgrimage. In order to serve this purpose, it must put mission over maintenance, it must give witness to the gospel through both evangelism and social action, and it must nurture its preparedness for mission by issuing battle commissions, providing training for mission, and organising its life in ways that enhance mission. It must never cease evaluating itself in the light of its mandate for mission.

5

Encamped for renewal

The nurturing community

The Church is a gathered community in which the missionary people of God encourage one another's spiritual growth and equip one another for mission.

TO say that the Church exists primarily for the sake of its mission in the world is in no way to question the importance of what takes place when the fellowship of believers gathers together. We have already said that the mission of the Church in the world is nothing other than the overflow of Christian caring within the Body of Christ (chapter 4). The gospel that is preached in word and deed in the world is the gospel that is formation of life. As the Church receives the gospel and is transformed by it, it becomes the missionary people of God: the mission of the Church is inextricably tied to the life of the fellowship. It is the natural expression of that life. Only as the Church is gathered for nurture can it be scattered for mission. Only as it worships can it serve. Only as it understands its relationship with God can it understand its relationship with the world. Only as it realises the reconciliation of life within itself can it preach reconciliation to the world. Only as it lives as a redemptive community can it speak of redemption for the human race.

The fellowship and the mission of the Church are two parts of one whole. Each needs the other in order for a congregation to fulfil its calling. Fellowship without mission dies of spiritual suffocation. Mission without fellowship dies of spiritual starvation. The fellowship of believers must live its life in and for the world, or it will die the natural death of the ingrown. The mission of the congregation must be strengthened, supported and resourced by the fellowship of believers, or it will be reduced to flurries of good works which fade because it has not been nurtured and reinforced from the home base.

Herein lies one of the key challenges of ecclesiastical leadership. Examples abound of congregations which die from the disease of insularism, as do examples of those who die because an ambitious service outreach in the larger community is carried out to the serious neglect of the nurturing and sustaining of the congregational fellowship itself. Often congregational leadership is polarised by those who, on the one hand, place primary importance on the internal life of the congregation and those, on the other hand, who place it on service to the community. The effective missionary leader will be able to integrate missionary and pastoral goals.[73]

This integration takes place when the reciprocal relationship between fellowship and mission becomes reality for the congregation. In chapter 2 we described the Church as a redemptive fellowship created by the Holy Spirit, and our focus was primarily on the life of the fellowship itself. But we also asserted that the redemptive life of the fellowship overflowed as a redemptive mission in the world. In this chapter we shall be concerned about developing an understanding of the Church which defines the specific relationship between fellowship and mission. We shall be seeing the Church as a company of pilgrims and an army at war who alternate between advancement on the field and encampment for rest, replenishment, renewal and revitalisation. As we have seen how the Church lives by accepting the reality of the Kingdom of God in its midst, so we shall now see how the life of the Church nurtures its proclamation of the Kingdom in the world. The nurture is provided through two basic ministries within the Church: the ministry of *encouragement* and the ministry of *equipping.*

The ministry of encouragement

Therefore encourage one another and build one another up . . . (1 Thessalonians 5:11). Just as in Christ the fullness of God was pleased to dwell (Colossians 1:19; 2:9), even so in the Church the fullness of Christ is pleased to dwell (Ephesians 1:23). As the body of Christ (1 Corinthians 12:27), or as members of Christ's body (Ephesians 5:30), or as the body of which Christ is Saviour (5:23) and head (Colossians 1:18), the Church is comprised of those who are at peace with God and man and therefore:

> . . . are no longer strangers and sojourners, but . . . fellow citizens with the saints and members of the household of God, built upon the foundation of the apostles and prophets, Christ Jesus himself being the cornerstone, in whom the whole structure is joined together and grows into a holy temple in the Lord; in whom [they] also are built into it for a dwelling place of God in the Spirit (Ephesians 2:19-22).

Here the risen Christ gives gifts for building up his body and equipping his saints (Ephesians 4:11, 12). So that he might fill all things (4:10) and unite all things in himself as God has purposed (1:9, 10), he has filled the Church with himself and his gifts. As such, the Church is the believer's natural support system.

(a) The Church as support system

Sociologists have amply demonstrated that human life and personality can be understood only in relation to the communities with which persons are associated during the course of their lives. Human development takes place in community, and personality is formed in part by the ways in which the individual interacts with and within the significant communities in his life.

James M. Gustafson has written a most helpful discussion on communities as the settings within which meaning, value and purpose become possible in human life.[74] According to him, *meaning* is related to the past: '. . . memory images come into consciousness according to the meaning they have for us'. *Value* is the category of the present: 'the unity of the dynamic present exists because it has meaning with reference to some value'. The future is understood in relation to the category of *purpose*: '. . . purpose is realised in the life of the future that possibly can emerge out of the present actuality'.[75] Gustafson speaks of the 'integrating centre of meaning' as the means by which past, present and future are brought together and interpreted in communities.

The Church is that community in which the meaning, value and purpose of Christian faith are interpreted in teaching, integrated in practice and celebrated in worship. It is where the faithful find encouragement by remembering God's gracious action in the past, by giving and receiving ministry and by sharing hopes for the future.

Communities have common experiences and memories which are essential to their continuity in time. These experiences and memories are the means by which shared meanings come into being. A community interprets its past, ascribing special significance to certain events, periods, struggles or accomplishments; remembers these by the preservation of tradition in the form of signs, formulations or histories; and celebrates them through rituals. This shared interpretation of the past is the process by which a community affirms and confirms what is meaningful to each individual, to the extent that he is a member of that community.

As a community of meaning, the Church is the place where Christians are *encouraged by remembrance.* Since the key to Christian remembering is the inspired Scriptures, the Scriptures are the primary source of encouragement (Romans 15:4). The preaching of the early Church began with remembrance of the Jewish past (Acts 7:2ff, etc), focused on remembrance of Jesus (2:22ff), and interpreted the life of Jesus as the fulfilment of the Jewish messianic promise (2:36; 1 Corinthians 15:3, 4). The four gospels are reliable remembrances of Jesus as Messiah. Often it is only in memory that we come to understand the true significance of persons and events. Jesus understood that his disciples did not grasp the deepest meaning of his life, teaching and death, but he trusted the Holy Spirit to work through their memory to bring understanding (John 14:26; 16:4-13). Writing to a persecuted Church, the author of the letter to the Hebrews brings to remembrance the enduring faith of their spiritual ancestors (Hebrews, chapter 11) as an encouragement to remain steadfast (12:1-3).

But the remembrance of events and persons that nurture our faith does not alone provide enough encouragement. Encouragement must also arise out of present circumstance and experience. As significant values are shaped and affirmed through interaction with significant people, they become the structure within which the present situation is perceived and interpreted by that community. As these values are shared and validated in interaction, persons find strength and support. It is in this sense that Christian values are upheld and reinforced in the shared life of the fellowship of believers. The Church, therefore, is a community of value where Christians are *encouraged by one another.*

The encouragement takes many forms. The community is encouraged by the faith of each member (Romans 1:12; 1 Thessalonians 3:7) and by the love of each for the other (Philemon 7). When support is needed, the fellowship responds (Galatians 6:1, 2; Colossians 4:11). When affliction strikes, the comfort of God is often mediated through the comfort of the community (2 Corinthians 1:3-7). Believers are admonished to encourage one another, to be on guard, and not be tempted to sin (Hebrews 3:13), and when one does fall, to forgive and encourage him (2 Corinthians 2:7). They are to help and uphold the weak (1 Thessalonians 5:14). The Church is a community of encouragement in which each member stands by the other and in so doing defines the value of Christian faith and fellowship.

But we must always remember that the Church is also on a pilgrimage; it is a community of purpose. As such, it is the place where Christians are *encouraged by the promise of a future.* This promised future is both temporal and eternal. The Church moves courageously forward in its mission because it comes under the order of the great commission (Matthew 28:18-20). There is to be no shirking this command; the Church is called to carry out Christ's mission. It is therefore the place of encouragement for Christian missioners (Acts 18:27). But the promised future is also eternal, and so the Church is also the place where believers are encouraged by the revelation of God's eternal purpose in human history through Christ (Ephesians 1:9, 10; Colossians 2:2, 3; 3:1-4).

As support system, then, the Church is where the fellowship of believers finds encouragement by remembering God's faithfulness, by giving and receiving ministry and by claiming the future which God has in store. It is where past, present and future come together and where the believer integrates them in terms of God's continuing purpose for human life. It is where the believer experiences the Kingdom, aligns himself with its agenda, and is emboldened to live and minister in the light of its bright reality. It is the place of encouragement.

(b) How the Church encourages

What are the means by which this encouragement takes place? There are four: worship, preaching, small group support and shepherding.

Worship begins with God. In both etymology and meaning, the word signifies 'worth-ship'. Worship therefore originates with the joyful recognition that God is worthy of our adoration and that all other worth derives from him. It is not surprising that Jesus' temptation in the wilderness reached its climax with Satan offering him 'all the kingdoms of the world and the glory of them . . . if you will fall down and worship me'. Jesus' ringing response, an allusion to Deuteronomy 6:13, is uncompromising:

> Begone, Satan! for it is written, 'You shall worship the Lord your God and him only shall you serve' (Matthew 4:10).

And so it is for Christ's body, the Church: for the Church integrity of worship is preserved by complete devotion to God's worth-ship. But God's worth-ship is not a mere abstraction for the Church. It is a reality that has been revealed in Jesus the Christ. The worth-ship of God is embodied in the Lordship of Jesus. Hence, John's beatific vision of heavenly worship shows God on the throne surrounded by adoring worshippers (Revelation, chapter 4), and then moves to adoration of the One who alone is qualified to open the scroll and break the seven seals—ie, carry out the plan of God in history (chapter 5).

> Worthy is the Lamb who was slain, to receive power and wealth and wisdom and might and honour and glory and blessing (5:12).

Worship centred on God revealed in Christ brings encouragement. In worship Christ becomes the High Priest through whom we

> draw near with a true heart in full assurance of faith, with our hearts sprinkled clean from an evil conscience and our bodies washed with pure water (Hebrews 10:22).

Here we find our confidence in God through Christ, here our sufficiency. Here also our qualification for ministry (2 Corinthians 3:4-6). In worship, therefore—in the presence of him who is worthy, through the mediation of Christ the Lord, by the power of the Holy Spirit—the Church is encouraged (given courage) to receive the Kingdom anew and pursue its missionary calling.

Preaching is another important means of encouragement. The apostle Paul reminded the Thessalonian Christians that the apostles had encouraged them by exhortation (1 Thessalonians 2:11), and explained to the Corinthian Church that the gift of prophecy, rightly used, brought 'upbuilding and encouragement and consolation' (1 Corinthians 14:3). Preaching is a part of worship and as such gives encouragement through interpretation of specific scriptural exhortation in dialogue with the congregation.[76]

All true biblical preaching brings encouragement. As Jesus 'came into Galilee, preaching the gospel of God' (Mark 1:14), so every Christian preacher is called by God to announce only that message which brings joy or carries the promise of fulfilment. Even the most prophetic sermons, even the sermons that announce God's judgment and bring uneasiness, even the sermons that invite hearers to face unpleasant realities in their lives, take their stand on the assurance of God's grace, and through that grace, on the promise that redemptive change and spiritual victory are real possibilities.

It is said that Karl Barth was once asked what his thick tomes of theology all boiled down to. With a teasing twinkle in his eyes, no doubt, but also with seriousness, he replied, 'Jesus loves me, this I know, for the Bible tells me so.' If this message is in fact true, if it is the central truth of the Scriptures, and if it lies at the heart of all true Christian theology, then encouragement is an important part of every sermon. No Christian sermon is without the liberating assurance of God's love in Christ and the power of this love to bring positive change.

Small groups are another important means of encouragement in the Church. In chapter 4 we described small groups as the settings in which persons struggle most decisively for healing, wholeness and community, and through personal growth and renewal are prepared for carrying out the Church's mission in the world. They have played a significant role in the Church throughout its history.[77] Jesus gathered around him a group of twelve men. He promised his disciples that 'where two or three are gathered in my name, there am I in the midst of them' (Matthew 18:20). First-century Christians gathered in house churches (small groups that met in homes) to search the Scriptures, study the apostles' teachings, share the common meal, support one another and pray together. Martin Luther conducted intimate 'table talks' with Christian friends. John Wesley's class meetings were, in the opinion of many, the most significant vehicle for spiritual revival and vitality in the 18th-century evangelical movement. And the 'brigades' of the early Salvationist movement were effective means not only for missionary outreach but also for nurture and fellowship.

In what ways can the small group become a means of encouragement? First, it can allow for a level of sharing which is impossible in the context of a larger congregation. Christ calls his Church neither to unchecked individualism nor to total conformism; he calls it to unity through diversity. This unity is achieved where members are affirmed in the richness of their differences and given the opportunity to exercise their respective gifts. It is best realised where small groups are a vital part of congregational life. The larger congregational setting does not allow for significant sharing and appreciation of differences; the smaller setting does. Members of small groups find encouragement as they become known and as they come to know others.

Second, the small group can become a means of encouragement through the acceptance of persons and the achievement of a high level of participation from members. Attitudes of prejudice and policies of discrimination tend to thrive where social distance is reinforced. They remain strong in the larger social context (including a large church) in which it is convenient to avoid the person who is different. But they are threatened in the small group setting where face-to-face confrontation is almost unavoidable and the opportunity for mutual appreciation greatly enhanced.[78] Also, persons who have not yet discovered or developed their gifts have far greater stimulus for doing so in the small group, where dormancy is more difficult to maintain and participation more strongly elicited.

Third, the small group can be a means of encouragement by developing patterns of Christian living and witness. Small groups tend to establish covenants and disciplines for themselves. A member's participation in the group tends to become untenable when he does not carry out the agreed-upon disciplines. Hence, in the Church the group functions as a community of accountability which encourages the member to commit himself to a lifestyle and discipline which will nurture spiritual growth, as well as equip for ministry. This kind of disciplining, this sustained commitment to a process of spiritual formation, cannot be effectively realised in the larger congregational setting. It must take place in small groups where encouragement comes through the strength and single-mindedness that purposeful discipline brings.

The fourth way in which the small group can be a means of encouragement is by fostering a climate for mutual burden bearing. The more intense interpersonal interaction level of the small group builds trust, heightens mutual concern, encourages unburdening, and increases readiness to assume a supportive role with others in the group. Group members often feel that they are pilgrimaging together and are happy to be able to rely on one another during this and other phases of the journey.

Fifth, the small group setting usually facilitates truthfulness grounded in love. It is difficult, and often inadvisable, to be truthful about personal struggles and failures before a larger group of people. Many will misunderstand, some will distort, and the response will often be superficial. The small group, on the other hand, has the capacity to nurture love, which in turn encourages honesty between members. When members feel accepted and supported, they risk truthfulness, and out of such truthfulness can come forgiveness and healing—and the encouragement to move ahead.

Let us summarise these five ways in which the small group can become a vehicle of encouragement by saying that it can serve as a kind of extended family within the congregation: a place of personal belonging where certain needs are met, personal growth is nurtured, members are respected and loved and empathy is felt. Members of the Church are brothers and sisters who have been adopted into the family through the redemption that is in Christ. They have passed from slavery under the law to sonship (family membership) in the household of faith. They are now full heirs of the promise and stand on the threshold of new possibilities (see Galatians 4:1-7). Through Christ they now value relationships—their relationship with God as Father, their relationship with fellow Christians as brothers and sisters—and they yearn and work for the extension of this family within the community of man (see 2 Corinthians 5:18-20).

It is our view that the Christian family can only be truly experienced in the smaller group setting. Confessing a familial oneness in Christ is one thing; living it out is another. The logistical impossibility of nurturing close relationships with every member of a medium- or large-size congregation is obvious. Small group settings within the congregation, however, afford the opportunity to experience the family of God in authentic ways. As such, their potential as a source of Christian encouragement is vast.

The final important means of encouragement in the Church is *shepherding.* The Scriptures refer to the Lord of the Church as 'that great Shepherd of the sheep' (Hebrews 13:20, *AV*) and 'the Shepherd and Bishop of your souls' (1 Peter 2:25, *AV*). Jesus himself used the shepherd and his sacrificial actions on behalf of the sheep as an analogy to interpret his own mission (John 10:1-16). The charge which he gave his disciples prior to sending them out on their mission included, along with preaching the Kingdom, meeting specific human needs: healing the sick, raising the dead, cleansing the lepers and casting out demons (Matthew 9:35-10:16).

The shepherding ministry of the Church, passed on from the first century to the present, can be summarily described by four functions: healing, sustaining, guiding and reconciling.[79] The healing function helps in the restoration to physical or emotional wholeness in such a way that spiritual development also results (see James 5:14-16). The sustaining function is the support of a person who is experiencing loss in some form, and its attendant pain, with a view toward personal and spiritual growth (see 1 Peter 1:3-9; 4:12-14; 5:10, 11). The guiding function consists in assisting perplexed persons to make choices that promote spiritual health and integrity (see Acts 20:28-31). The reconciling function aims at the re-establishment of broken relationships between both God and man and man and man, with the understanding that each of these two basic relationships is always integrally related to the other (see Ephesians 2:11-22).

It can readily be seen that each of these functions of shepherding comes into play in ministering to persons who are experiencing some form of crisis—illness, loss, perplexity or enmity. In each of these cases, the ministry of the shepherd is a source of encouragement. This is not to say that his role is to cheer people up; it is far more difficult. It is to stand by the person in crisis, in some way to experience the crisis with him, to challenge him to spiritual growth and, in this way, to help mediate God's redemptive presence. This kind of ministry does not deal in merely trying to brighten up someone's day; it deals in brightening up his future by facilitating positive personal change in the present. It brings real encouragment because it builds courage.

Who is it that carries out this ministry? Those who have been given the gifts and are willing to exercise them in responsible ways. They are ordained ministers and trained lay persons who take the priesthood of all believers seriously (see chapter 3) and have answered their call to shepherding others on behalf of the one 'great Shepherd of the sheep'. By virtue of training and experience, the pastor or priest of the congregation is usually more skilled in shepherding; but the lay person may have spiritual endowments and maturity that can be used to bring courage to brothers and sisters in crisis. Any congregation in which the shepherding is done only by the ordained minister is not receiving enough encouragement.[80] Conversely, where the people who are gifted with caring are putting their gift to use in ministry, the congregation is not only supported but also challenged to claim the future.

(c) Keeping encouragement alive

How does the Church promote the ministry of encouragement and challenge members to cultivate the gift? How can it celebrate this ministry in such a way as to affirm it and stimulate its multiplication?

First, in its public gatherings the local congregation can not only celebrate the encouragement of the gospel but also promote the ministry of encouragement among members and in the world. Sermons, for example, can challenge believers both to encourage one another's spiritual growth and to bring the message of hope to those people who live in despair. Public prayer, by inviting the people of God to perceive and claim his saving involvement in their lives, can give them courage and strengthen their resolve to be encouragers. Celebrations of unity in Christ—like the love feast—can reveal the reality of Christ's body for the Church as a basis for support and can motivate mutual encouragement. Celebrations of the Church's servant calling—like footwashing, the sacrament of servant-hood—can, by stimulating loving service, nourish the attitudes and actions of encouragement.

Second, there can be structured ways of promoting the ministry of encouragement. Some congregations have pastoral care or shepherding groups which recruit, train and mobilise members with the gift of encouragement. These groups usually work very closely with the pastor so that the shepherding ministry is one ministry of the congregation and a continuing expression of the encouragement of the gospel in the life of that fellowship.

Whatever the ways and means of promoting it, the Church must keep alive the ministry of encouragement or it will have no basis for its mission. Encouragement produces courage, and courage produces action; discouragement produces timidity, and timidity produces inertia. The mission of the Church is actually built on encouragement.

Let us now turn our attention to how the Church nurtures its proclamation of the gospel in the world through the ministry of equipping.

The ministry of equipping

And he gave [gifts] . . . for the equipping of the saints for the work of service, to the building up of the body of Christ . . . (Ephesians 4:11, 12, NAS). The ministry of equipping is the means by which the body of Christ prepares itself for service within and outside the fellowship. Some gifts of the Spirit are more suited to ministry within the congregation (eg, teaching), some to outreach (eg, evangelism) and some to both (eg, practical service). All of them, when exercised, contribute to the mission of the congregation by building up the body and providing resources for outreach.

The congregation is *an equipping centre.* It is the place where members are helped to discover, develop and deploy their gifts for ministry. Discovery requires the recognition that every Christian has one or more gifts for ministry and that there can be no discrimination—by sex, social status or race—in providing opportunities for each one to develop his gift and deploy it effectively (see 1 Corinthians 7:7; 12:4ff). Development requires the recognition that gifts must be nurtured if they are to reach their promise, and the willingness to be committed to the discipline of training (see 1 Timothy 4:14, 15; 2 Timothy 1:6). Deployment requires the recognition that all gifts for ministry are given for the purpose of enabling the Church to realise its calling, and the courage actually to risk offering one's gift in acts of ministry (see Romans 12:6ff; 1 Peter 4:10, 11).

(a) How the Church equips

There are a number of ways in which the local congregation prepares and trains its members for ministry. Some of them can be effective in challenging members to discover their gifts and seek to understand their application in the life and mission of the congregation. Study of the Scriptures, for example, can bring not only encouragement but also guidance in the recognition and utilisation of spiritual gifts.[81] Worship can be planned and conducted in such a way as to deal with the affirmation and the employment of gifts as an essential aspect of response to God's action and call in Christ. Instruction about the utilisation of gifts for ministry can be given in sermons, special Christian education classes, regular congregational meetings (soldiers' meetings), and recruits' or information classes for those who are interested in the implications of membership of the Body of Christ.

But the Church is charged by its Lord not only to help members discover their gifts for ministry but also to stimulate and guide in the development of those gifts. The local congregation is, indeed, a centre for the equipping of the saints for the work of ministry, and as such responds to the challenge to provide the structure for training. The means of gift development may take different forms, including special training classes/workshops for specific lay ministries, leadership seminars, apprenticeships with more experienced lay persons or even the pastor, and structured opportunities to reflect on and learn from events from one's actual ministry. It should also be remembered that gift development is a continuing process. Ministry stagnation can easily set in not only when gifts once utilised become dormant but also when skills are used but not continually honed. The congregation that is effectively equipping for ministry is the congregation that is always in the process of training.

The small group can serve very effectively as a setting for ministry equipping. In chapter 4 we described the strengths of the small group as a vehicle for implementing the Church's mission (mission team), and earlier in the present chapter its value as a place of encouragement. We now assert that the mission team model is also well suited as a vehicle for gift development. By definition, the mission team will have a clear purpose and specific goals and will therefore tend more readily to identify the gifts needed to reach the goals. Because it is difficult to hide in a small group and because the tasks of small groups usually require unanimous involvement if they are to be carried out effectively, members of mission teams are likely to be challenged to claim their ministry gifts and develop them for those tasks. There is also a built-in accountability factor in the small group: face-to-face meetings, periodic reporting to colleagues, group pressure. More importantly, the group is a powerful support system for encouraging members to realise their potential in both developing and deploying gifts for ministry.[82]

(b) Blessing and supporting the equipped

In what way does the Church reinforce the ministry of

equipping the saints, as well as celebrate milestones of training for those who have reached an important level of preparedness and are ready to assume specific responsibilities? The answer is through some act of commissioning those who have prepared themselves for specific responsibilities in the life or mission of the Church. We have already seen (chapter 3) that in The Salvation Army both officers (full-time ministers) and local officers (lay leaders) are commissioned to the ministry to which they have been called. The commissioning is a public recognition by the denomination and its local congregation—as concrete, historical expressions of the Church—of specific callings and the completion of adequate preparation. It is also an opportunity to reinforce the calling of all Christians to utilise their gifts for ministry and the responsibility of the Church to recognise gifts and open all ministries, without artificial discriminations, to all qualified persons in the denomination or congregation.

When the resurrected Jesus was about to ascend, he charged his disciples with their mission to preach his name to all nations as faithful witnesses. Then he led them out to Bethany and, lifting his hands, blessed them (Luke 24:44-51). Their equipping for ministry was not yet complete, but they had been with Jesus for many months and Jesus was now ready to entrust his mission to them. He knew that the Holy Spirit would come and continue the teaching process (John 14:25, 26). He knew that the disciples would edify and train one another. So he gave his blessing.

In a similar way, as the Body of Christ, as the continuation of Christ's visible presence in the world, the Church recognises the blessing of its Lord on those who have prayerfully and diligently prepared for ministries to which they have been called. It is free to give this blessing itself because it does so in response to the blessing which its Lord has already given. It is marking the commencement of a pilgrimage in service and offering its continual support to a ministry which it has endorsed. It is celebrating the joy of service. It is blessing and supporting those who have equipped themselves.

Encouraging and equipping the missionary Church

At the beginning of this chapter we pointed out that the mission of the Church was inextricably tied to the life of the fellowship and was, in fact, dependent upon it. Now, at the close of the chapter, we must come back to this truth. The missionary Church needs to hear it again and again. Salvationists need to hear it. The denomination or local congregation which gives priority to mission must take special care to nurture itself and build the fellowship. Otherwise, missionary vitality will be lost.

Let us now summarise the ways in which this loss can occur. First, obsession with the missionary battle can so monopolise the thinking and doing of a congregation that insufficient investment is made in nurturing the personal spiritual life of members and the corporate life of the fellowship. The importance of one's personal pilgrimage and the communion of saints is lost. So much is invested in serving the world's needy that too little is left over for responding to the growth needs and the hurts of those within the fellowship. Eventually, mission practitioners become spiritual dwarfs through lack of proper sustenance, and the congregation's witness and service in the world shrivel to perfunctory action.

Second, the functional, task-oriented mind-set which is characteristic of many congregations oriented primarily to mission can clearly work to the detriment of personal relationships. It is possible for 'encouragement' to be seen primarily as pep talks and praise sessions for motivating members to work harder; and for 'equipping' to be devoted almost exclusively to cultivating talents and skills to enable the congregation to perform its services for the community. The role of the small group can diminish as congregations become obsessed with tasks and ignore interaction and process. Small groups that do exist can become mere task forces with little attention to the growth needs of participants. Authentic shepherding—shepherding that goes beyond obligatory hospital visits—can become a lost art.[83] A congregation can become starved for community—and die from a lack of it.

Third, the task-oriented congregation can become so obsessed with achievement that it gives solid support only to the achievers. Encouragement becomes a function of success and is given only when success is achieved or clearly in sight. It is not seen as an ongoing ministry in which God is trusted for the outcome, but rather as a means to the organisational end. It is unable to provide support at the deeper levels of spiritual pilgrimage, where respite from the battle is sometimes needed; rather, it only supports 'productivity'. Short-range goals, which promise quick gratification, replace commitment to long-range purposes, whose pursuits can lead to real fruit bearing. Productivity, then, replaces fruitfulness; achievers replace fruit-bearers. The future is sacrificed for the present.

Fourth and lastly, the mission obsessed congregation can lose its joy and spontaneity. The mission of the Church is not primarily a task to be performed, although it is demanding work. It is the overflow of congregational caring. It is the good news of Jesus Christ bursting the Church's seams and pouring out into the world. It is no accident that in the days of the Army's greatest missionary vitality, the movement was known by all as a joyous group with infectious enthusiasm.

By this reputation is the missionary Church always known. As the congregation gathers together and receives afresh the new Kingdom in Christ, members are ignited with missionary fire. The joy of the Kingdom is contagious. The missionary Church is the gathered Church infecting the world with joy.

6

Committed to the future

The colony of hope

The Church is the eschatological community that prays for the coming Kingdom and lives in the light of its dawning.

THE missionary Church is the Church of the future; the traditionalist Church is the Church of the past. The congregation that has lost its mission is the congregation that has found maintenance, and preoccupation with the maintenance of traditions undermines the real value of ecclesiastical tradition, which is the preservation of the purpose and calling of the Church. The Church's enduring tradition is mission; it is a dynamic tradition that challenges the Church courageously to open itself to God's future, as did the 'cloud of witnesses' who went before. The missionary Church looks backward so that it can confidently step forward.

As the new humanity which has been chartered by Christ, the Church has entered the Kingdom of God which will be consummated in the future. As the redemptive fellowship which has been created by the Holy Spirit, it strains toward the time when all things will be reconciled in Christ. As the pilgrim people who have been called to a journey, it is always moving into the future. As the army of salvation which has been commissioned for battle, it is never at rest, always preparing for a future battle, so long as humanity is oppressed by sin. And as the nurturing community which is encamped for renewal, it encourages and equips itself for the future. The missionary Church keeps its eye on the breaking dawn of the Kingdom's consummation.

The Bible is a book of the future. The Old Testament is saturated with the promise of the future (see Jeremiah chapter 31). It strains toward the day when the brokenness of nations and the sin of the human heart will be healed (see Isaiah chapters 55, 56). The prophet Jeremiah is a good example of this confidence in the future. With the enemy about to take Jerusalem, he went out and purchased a field! The Israelite nation was about to fall apart, and he made an *investment* in it. By any practical standard, it was a foolish act, a crazy scheme. But Jeremiah believed that God would once again bring blessing and prosperity, and he was willing at personal cost to lay that hope on the line (Jeremiah chapter 32). The prophets promised a new Kingdom.

The New Testament witnesses to Jesus as the Messiah in whom the promised Kingdom is realised. '. . . if it is by the finger of God that I cast out demons, then the Kingdom of God has come upon you,' said Jesus (Luke 11:20). The apostle Paul held that '. . . in Christ God was reconciling the world to himself . . .' (2 Corinthians 5:19). But even though the Kingdom had come, it had not been consummated. Hence, the disciples are commanded by their resurrected Lord to 'go . . . and make disciples of all nations . . .' (Matthew 28:19). The mission of the Church is based upon the future of the Kingdom, the vision of 'a new heaven and a new earth' (Revelation 21:1), the coming together of those from the east and the west to sit down at the Kingdom table (Matthew 8:11). Like growing things the Kingdom will develop from a small kernel into a full plant. The purpose of the Church's mission is to nurture that future.

The starting point, of course, is the Church itself. In its own life and work, the Church must be open to God's future. It must demonstrate the future so that it can point the world to the future. For this reason it is the eschatological[84] community that not only *prays* for the Kingdom to come but also *lives* in the light of its dawning. In prayer the Church looks to God's future in Christ and longs for its fulfilment. In its living the Church opens the present to the transforming invasion of God's future. The Church prays and lives as a colony of hope that is committed to the coming future in Christ.

The future of the Church

In order to speak of the Church of the future, we must first speak of the future of the Church. What *is* the future toward which the Church is moving? What is the promise for the world which it has claimed? Where is the Church heading? For what is it praying? The answer to this question, the question of the future of the Church, leads to the answer to the question of how the Church is to live its life in the world today: it lives its life in active anticipation of God's future, it seizes the hope in the present, it is the Church of the future. What, then, is the future which the Church claims and which thereby becomes the basis for its own life and mission?

It is the consummation of all history in the triumph of the grace of God in Christ Jesus. It is the historical realisation of the work of the atonement, bringing history as we know it to an end. While it is not an irresistible consequence for each individual, so that freedom is not forfeited, it is the completion of God's saving act for the world in which all of fallen creation participates (Romans 8:19ff). It is the climax of salvation history described by John the Divine:

> Then I saw a new heaven and a new earth; for the first heaven and the first earth had passed away. . . . And I saw the holy city, new Jerusalem, coming down out of heaven from God, prepared as a bride adorned for her husband; and I heard a loud voice from the throne saying, 'Behold, the dwelling of God is with men. He will dwell with them, and they shall be his people, and God himself will be with them; he will wipe away every tear from their eyes, and death shall be no more, neither shall there be mourning nor crying nor pain any more, for the former things have passed away' (Revelation 21:1-4).

The Church is passionately committed to this hope as the decisive reality that was promised in the cross (Colossians 1:20) and will be consummated in the fullness of time (Ephesians 1:9, 10). It is a hope that creates a distinctive ecclesiastical character. We shall now develop that character as freedom from the oppressive past, courage for the promised future and hope for the whosoever.

(a) Freedom from the oppressive past

We have spoken of the Church as a pilgrim people on the move to God's future and in the process of freeing themselves from the oppression of the *status quo* (chapter 3). We now want to establish the objective ground of its willingness to leave behind the stifling entanglements of the past, and then briefly to describe the character of this freedom.

The Church finds its objective ground in the gospel of Jesus as the Christ. What the gospel proclaims as the new reality in Jesus Christ, the Church, which is comprised of those who respond to this reality in faith, claims as the basis for its being and doing. Jesus preached an ethic that is intelligible only in the context of the presence of a radically new and different Kingdom (see Matthew chapters 5-7). He recognised that even though the redemptive life that he had come to bring was actually the fulfilment of the Old Testament law's deepest intention for human life (5:17), it would not be able to stay in the moulds of the old order (9:16, 17). In the light of the Kingdom's dawning, the moulds are, in fact, exposed as inadequate for holding the new future. They must be left behind.

The old moulds are many things that are waiting to be superseded. They are attitudes and actions that are rendered insufficient in the gospel of Jesus. One example is found in this statement of Jesus:

> You have heard that it was said, 'You shall love your neighbour and hate your enemy.' But I say to you, love your enemies and pray for those who persecute you (5:43, 44).

The old moulds are also institutions and structures that are not capable of containing the liberating spirit of the new gospel, like the Jerusalem Temple of Jesus' day whose end he foresaw (24:1, 2). And there are also prejudices that contradict the new social relationships that are in Christ (Galatians 3:28).

Founded on the proclamation of this new order which the old order cannot contain, the true Church accepts the challenge of breaking out of old confining moulds which do not allow the gospel to do its work. It claims its freedom from the oppressive past. The future belongs to the new order.

The apostle Paul saw the future of the gospel and recognised that the mould of Jewish provincialism and legalism could not contain it. The Protestant Reformers saw in that future the triumph of saving grace and recognised that medieval schemes of meritorious salvation contradicted it. Wesley saw in it a Church of spiritual integrity and vitality and knew full well that parochial establishmentarianism stifled it. Booth saw in it the realisation of God's universal redemptive plan in Christ and realised that ecclesiastical provincialism hindered it.

Taking its stand in the future of the gospel, the Church finds liberation from traditions that oppress and from oppressions that have become traditionalised. As a people on the move and as an army at war, it shakes off impediments and weights that immobilise. It cuts the cords of fear and finds courage for the promised future.

(b) Courage for the promised future

The Bible is not only a book of the future, it is also a book of victory. It reveals God's future as the triumph of his saving plan in Christ. The prophets foresaw victory. Isaiah, for example, deriding the Babylonian gods for their anaemic failure to deliver the future, proclaims a God who, having spoken, would bring his words to pass, who, having purposed, would do it (Isaiah 46). Here is what he will do:

> I bring near my deliverance, it is not far off,
> and my salvation will not tarry;
> I will put salvation in Zion,
> for Israel my glory (46:13).

The Church sees in the person and work of Christ the triumph of God's purpose in history. In Christ it sees this triumph not as the ascendency of the Jewish nation but as the disarmament of all of sin's oppressive forces in the cross (Colossians 2:15) and the subsequent movement of history toward the fullness of time when that victory would be consummated in the union of all things in him (Ephesians 1:10). This is God's purpose, and it can be relied upon. Writing to a discouraged and persecuted church, the author of the letter to the Hebrews urges his readers, with him, 'to seize the hope set before us' (Hebrews 6:18).

Hence, the Church is the eschatological community that has thrown in its future lot with the hope that is in Christ. It seeks, sees and seizes the future. It sometimes acts outlandishly because God's future is discontinuous with many structures and policies of the present world order—including some that are ecclesiastical—and the Church must give witness to where God is leading. It does so at some risk: the present world order fears and attempts to forestall the future, thus placing in jeopardy those who will fight for it. There is no way the Church of the future can be timid. The future calls for courage.

The early Salvationist mission was the product of courageous hearts committed to the promised future. If some of its outlandishness was the expression of misguided enthusiasm, most of it was undoubtedly action parables of the future and crusades to allow the future to shape the present. The campaigns to end the entrapment of minors for prostitution in London, to wipe out the heinous French penal colony on Devil's Island, to cross cultural and caste boundaries in India, to proclaim the gospel in public places at the frequent risk of arrest and abuse, to assist poor people in building the foundation for a hopeful tomorrow, to challenge the wrecks of humanity to become new creatures in Christ—all of this, and more, was done with an eye to the future. All, at personal risk. The Church that commits itself to God's future is characterised by courage in the present, courage to take the less-travelled road, to invest time and energy in what is of eternal significance, to seek the Kingdom of God and his righteousness, to live by hope, to share the hope. It is the courage to stand where Commissioner Frederick Booth-Tucker, early Salvationist leader, stood when he wrote:

> . . . as we contemplate the future, how glorious, how far-reaching, how world-embracing, how Niagara-like in their proportions are the prospects that God's own hand has spread before us. Like Moses, we view a very Canaan of hope and help, of holy warfare and happy victory stretching out before us. Oh, that we may keep our eyes and hearts fixed upon the fight! Oh, that we may be enabled to turn a deaf ear to the world's clamours which would call us in one way or another to sacrifice our privileges for some will-o'-the-wisp phantom, in chasing which we should lose the substantial realities God has placed within our reach![85]

(c) Hope for the whosoever

The future to which the Church is committed is a Kingdom that includes all nations, races, classes and cultures. Like that of the Jewish nation (Isaiah 49:6), the destiny of the Church is wrapped up in the future of universal salvation in Christ, and this future marks the character of the Church and its mission. When the world sees the Church, it should see hope for the whosoever.

The inclusive gospel has been a watchword of the Salvationist movement. In focusing on the poor and dispossessed, the Army was including those who were usually the first to be excluded. That is why mission based upon the gospel invalidates itself if it does not include them; that is why every local congregation which bases its existence and purpose on this gospel should in some crucial way tie itself to mission among them. The future of the inclusive gospel demands it.

The poor, more than any other group of people, are those

without hope. They live from day to day and are uncertain about tomorrow. The New Testament gospel was preached especially to them, and it sounded the note of hope (Luke 4:18). They were told of the Christ who had come to set them free, the Christ who would come again to establish his righteous Kingdom (Revelation 11:15), the Christ in whom all things in heaven and earth would be united (Ephesians 1:10). The image of the coming Christ became a powerful symbol in the early Church.

But it was not a symbol of postponement. The Christ who was to come in fullness at the end of time was also the Christ who came now. The hope given in Christ was a hope that was already at work transforming people's lives. The Church was therefore given the task of searching for, and working towards, the reconciled life and the reconciliation of life characteristic of the Kingdom (1 Thessalonians 5:1-11); and those who responded to the gospel received hope not only for the future but also for the transformation of the present. Only in this way could the gospel really be for the whosoever. Only in this way could everyone be included. To consign the poor to a hopeless existence in the present world order, to be exchanged for bliss at the end of time, is to use eschatology to rationalise the inequities of the social order and to opt for an unbiblical gnostic type of salvation.[86]

The Salvation Army gave the Victorian working man a hope that centred both on a heavenly and on an earthly Kingdom. The Kingdom hereafter was promised to the convert, but the Kingdom of Christ *here* also became a consuming passion for William Booth. He was profoundly moved by the hopeless condition of the abject poor. He set his movement to the task of offering them the opportunity to improve their earthly lot. Hence the comprehensive social scheme of 1890.[87]

As the eschatological community that prays for the coming Kingdom, the Church is given the vision to see redemptive possibilities everywhere. It is not a futuristic community that has opted out of the present for the sake of a postponed, peremptory second coming. Rather, it sees the second coming as the consummation of the ongoing transformations of Christ in the world. At prayer, the Church is given the vision to see Christ at work for the whosoever. At work, it responds to the vision. In the words of Catherine Booth:

> . . . there are thousands talking about his (Christ's) 'second coming' who will neither see nor receive him in the person of his humble and persecuted followers. Christ manifested in the flesh, vulgar flesh,

> they cannot receive. No: they are looking for him in the clouds! What a sensation there would be if he were to come again in a carpenter's coat! How many would recognise him then, I wonder? I am afraid it would be the old story, 'Crucify him!' 'Away with him!' 'Whoever denieth that Jesus *is* come (not *did* come) in the flesh is antichrist.' Oh, for grace always to see him where he is to be seen, for, verily, flesh and blood doth not reveal this unto us! Well, bless the Lord, *I keep seeing him risen again in the forms of drunkards and ruffians of all description*[88] (last italics mine).

In seeing and responding to the vision of Christ as the hope for the whosoever, the Church is allowing itself to be moulded by God's future.

The Church of the future

As the community of believers who are committed to and moulded by God's future, the Church is a colony of hope in a world of despair. It is the Kingdom colonising itself throughout the land in the form of specific settlements (local congregations) that live their life in accord with homeland citizenship and invite others to join the colony. It is the fellowship of those who courageously live in the light of the Kingdom's dawning and urge those who live in darkness to see the light. It is the Church of the future that points the world to the future.

The future, therefore, dominates the life of the Church. What the Church *is* can only be understood in relation to the future of its becoming; what it *does* is rightfully done only with an eye to the future of its mission. God's future in Christ dominates the lifestyle, fellowship, mission and structure of the Church. In this way the Church is a colony of hope in the world that gives witness to what the future has in store.

(a) The future in lifestyle

The Church is not called to live in the future but rather to let the future live in the present. It is not called to cut all ties with the past and rush willy-nilly into the future but rather to claim the future as the fulfilment of what God has promised and made possible in the past. To claim God's future in this way results in a style and structure of life which takes that future seriously and allows it to shape the way life is lived.

What, then, *is* the lifestyle of the Church of the future? The answer is *stewardship.*

Stewardship is the faithful management of life in accord with

God's future. God reveals his own stewardship in Christ 'as a plan [*oikonomia* = stewardship] for the fulness of time, to unite all things in him [Christ], things in heaven and things on earth' (Ephesians 1:10). As a community committed to this universal stewardship plan, the Church has a corresponding plan. It consists in the management of its life in response to God's future in Christ. Focusing on this future, it draws all decisions and actions into the eschatological image that the Christian hope upholds. The Church's stewardship, therefore, is the conformity of its planning and living to the destiny of all creation.

What this means is that stewardship, in the final analysis, is not merely the wise management of resources, as in good business practice. Rather, it is the discovery of the promise of the future in everyday living and response to that promise in lifestyle. The lifestyle of the Church courageously reflects the future. It is stewardship in the present that has its eye on the realisation of God's stewardship plan for the future.

Hence, in 'redeeming the time' (Colossians 4:5, *AV*), the Church is not merely practising wise time management; it is using its time as a gift from God to be employed redemptively for the transformation of the present in the light of God's future (3:1-4). In employing gifts for one another (1 Peter 4:10), it is neither putting its endowments on display nor strengthening its worldly appeal; it is seeing the completion of God's plan (4:7) and building up the life and mission of the body so that Jesus may be glorified and his eternal dominion affirmed (4:11). And in responsibly managing its material resources, it is not building its own kingdom of institutional security and political strength; it is risking what God has entrusted by investing it by faith in what God will do (Matthew 25:14-30).

In this sense stewardship is the Church's lifestyle. It is a lifestyle that is based upon, and is the expression of, the good news of 'your Father's good pleasure to give you the kingdom' (Luke 12:32). In *this* Kingdom the Church finds its hope, and therefore its security. In *this* Kingdom it invests all its resources. In *this* Kingdom it finds the worthwhile treasures of the heart and the strength to divest itself of the corruptible (12:33, 34). Stewardship is the lifestyle of those who seek first the Kingdom and are content to let everything else be addition (12:31).

Stewardship becomes reality when the freedom of the gospel finds expression in the discipline of the Church. If it was *for* freedom that Christ set the Church free, then the Church must be willing to live its life in a way that rejects any return to law's enslavement (Galatians 5:1). What this requires is a lifestyle that is focused on the new future and is free from the old futilities. It requires discipline. As an important characteristic of the pilgrim lifestyle (chapter 3), discipline is the means by which disciples are able to focus their lives on the Kingdom. It is the means by which the unimportant is put aside for the sake of the important and the good is put aside for the sake of the better. Without it, the Church can never really receive the Kingdom; lesser realities will be substituted, counterfeits will be embraced. As a steward of freedom, the Church lives a disciplined life.[89]

(b) The future in fellowship

In chapter 2 we described the Church as a fellowship created by the Holy Spirit and empowered by the Spirit for redemptive living, and in chapter 3 as a pilgrim people on the move. In chapter 4 we saw how this mobile, transformed community is a missionary army that adapts itself to the battle terrain and to the culture of the people it is seeking to reach in mission. We shall now see how the future toward which the Church is moving actually shapes the character and culture of the fellowship itself. We shall do so by focusing on three important ways in which this future becomes a norm for the contemporary Church as it overcomes cultural, social and economic barriers to fellowship in Christ.

The first important way in which the Church overcomes barriers to fellowship is by *opening itself to the poor.*[90] Jesus announced that with his coming the poor now had the gospel preached to them (Luke 7:22). He once suggested that he was especially incarnate in the persons of the poor and oppressed and that the ministry of his true followers therefore related to them in a decisive way (Matthew 25:31ff). The Christian Church was originally comprised mainly of the less privileged, the outcasts and the disinherited. They, it seems, were the most receptive to the gospel.

If the gospel, then, is to be preached to the poor in particular, the congregation that ignores them is violating this gospel. If the Christ beckons his followers to discover his presence in the form of the outcast, then the congregation which excludes the outcast, whether overtly or subtly, is weaving a social fabric that effectively obscures the gospel. Every congregation which bases its existence and purpose on the inclusive gospel must in some crucial way tie itself to mission among the poor and to a hospitable fellowship within which the poor find community in Christ.[91]

What are some of the ways in which the Church opens itself to the poor? It does so, first of all, by offering *hope.* As we have seen, this hope is for both the hereafter and the here. The Church of the future risks opening itself to God's promises, proclaiming the future in Christ and building hope for the despairing. Booth's great social scheme was an attempt to create a massive plan for making a new beginning possible for the abject poor. He sincerely believed it would work, were adequate financial backing to be given. Support was received, but it was insufficient to fund the entire plan. Hence, the plan failed as a comprehensive scheme. But the hope has remained, and the missionary Church continues to ignore the counsel of despair and the risk of optimistic involvement.

Another way in which the Church opens itself to the poor is to *adapt* itself to their culture. The apostle Paul spoke of the necessity of becoming 'all things to all men' in order that he might 'by all means save some' (see 1 Corinthians 9:19-23). In order to win Jews he became as a Jew, and in order to win Gentiles he became as a Gentile. He proved that the gospel was culturally adaptable. The gospel could not really be preached to the Gentiles until there could be a Gentile Church.

Similarly, the early Church could not authentically preach to the poor unless it was willing to be the Church in which the poor could find full membership and participation. Its success in this endeavour can be attested by the objection frequently levelled against it by its cultured pagan critics to the effect that it was comprised mainly of insignificant people.[92] Paul reminded his Corinthian readers:

> . . . consider your call, brethen; not many of you were wise according to worldly standards, not many were powerful, not many were of noble birth . . . (1 Corinthians 1:26).

The majority of early Salvationists were also socially insignificant people. It was intended that they should be. The movement was for the poor. But this intention could be carried out only if drastic measures were taken to identify with the poor, to reach them where they were and on their own terms. The established Victorian churches were ill-equipped to do so; they were too deeply rooted in the respectable *status quo.*

Hence, the Salvationist movement developed a strategy for

adapting to the working class culture. It began with the willingness to abandon respectability. Because the Victorian Church was generally perceived as a respectable social institution which was attended by and seemingly designed for the middle and upper classes,[93] the working man considered himself excluded. There was really no place for him in church. It was therefore a missionary imperative that the Salvationist movement break with 'respectable religion' and establish a bond with proletarian culture. In a letter to James Jeremy in Cleveland, William Booth wrote that the great curse of the contemporary churches was respectability and that he had decided to throw it overboard.[94] That the strategy worked is well attested by the evidence. In a public meeting in March of 1880, the rector of Falmouth said:

> There ought to be a section of The Salvation Army in every town in the kingdom where there were over 5,000 persons, because they reached men and women whom church and chapel people . . . could not get at.[95]

Specific aspects of the Army's strategy of adaptation to the culture and terrain of the poor have been described in chapter 4. We view these as one expression of the missionary Church's intention to overcome barriers to fellowship by opening itself to the poor and by accepting the consequences of this departure from respectable religion.

A third way in which the Church opens itself to the poor is by *eliminating* the climate and practice of *socio-economic discrimination.* When Bramwell Booth sought to arrange a worship service for Salvationists at St Paul's Cathedral, Dean Church became anxious and inquired if most Salvationists wore the hob-nailed boots that were the usual footwear of working people. When an affirmative answer was given, the Dean announced that the service could not be held; St Paul's had just been repaired at considerable cost, and the marble might be scratched.[96] Denied a place in the established community of God's people and at the Lord's table, the poor who sought faith usually went elsewhere. Many of them came to The Salvation Army, where they sang:

> I'm at home in the Army
> More than I am anywhere.
> You can dress as you like,
> You can sit where you like,
> You're all quite equal there. . . .

A fourth way in which the Church opens itself to the poor is by *providing specific communities* to which they can belong and in which they can actively participate. In general, the Victorian churches offered only low profile and passive membership to the working man. There were few groups of people to which the poor could comfortably belong. The Army, on the other hand, formed 'brigades', groups which had assigned tasks to perform but which also became more intimate communities in which members shared their lives and lent support to one another. These brigades or work forces became the means by which the working class convert was incorporated into the body and often became a lay leader.

The missionary Church has always found ways to open itself to the poor.

A second important way in which it overcomes barriers to fellowship is by *opening ministry and leadership to women.* The relatively prominent place of women in the New Testament Church and the assertion by the apostle Paul that in Christ there is 'neither male nor female' (Galatians 3:28) are nothing short of revolutionary in the light of the first-century view of the status of women in society and religion. But since that time, it has taken many centuries for the Church to take seriously again the equal birthright of women in the gospel by opening itself to female leadership and ordination.

The Salvationist movement has played its part in this revolution. Officership (full-time ministry) was open to women early on,[97] thanks especially to the unmistakable leadership gifts and sanctified courage of Catherine Booth. In a pamphlet on women's ministry published in 1859, Mrs Booth wrote:

> Whether the Church will allow women to speak in *her* assemblies can only be a question of time; common sense, public opinion, and the blessed results of female agency will force her to give an honest and impartial rendering of the solitary text on which she grounds her prohibitions. Then, when the true light shines, and God's words take the place of man's traditions, the Doctor of Divinity who shall teach that Paul commands woman to be silent when God's Spirit urges her to speak, will be regarded much the same as we should regard an astronomer who should teach that the sun is the earth's satellite.[98]

In 1890, on her deathbed, she penned what were probably her last words on behalf of eliminating sexism in ministry and Church leadership. The letter was to the Army's first woman divisional commander (district superintendent), Captain Polly

Ashton, newly appointed. In it are found these words of encouragement:

> . . . I wish . . . that (your promotion) may help forward that honourable and useful employment of my own sex in the Master's service, which I have so strongly desired and laboured for, and of which I have been enabled in some measure, by the mercy of God, to be an example.[99]

As the fellowship that opens itself to the future, the missionary Church understands that the duality of sex is not a duality of ministry or leadership and it sees clearly that God's future has no place for the oppressions of sexist culture. As a branch of the Church that came to this understanding and vision over a hundred years ago, the Army must be careful not to regress through the infiltration of cultural prejudice. The Church as a whole must be willing to be courageous and prophetic in this matter. Sexism has no future in Christ, and the extent to which the Church allows it is the extent to which, in this regard, it resists God's future.

The third important way in which the Church overcomes barriers to fellowship is by *opening itself to children.* Cultural religion is typically an adult affair in which children are given insignificant roles and are looked upon as passive learners who, when they have learned the dogma from adults and have reached the predetermined threshold to adulthood, are admitted into the religious fellowship. The missionary Church, on the other hand, sees that God's future in Christ involves a radical transformation in how children are viewed and appreciated.

First, they are looked upon as models of *openness* and *responsiveness* (see Mark 10:13-16). Adult culture values realism and pragmatism. It accepts the givenness of the present world order and dreams for no more than to improve upon it. It conditions us to respond in programmed ways. Within this mind-set there is no opening for spontaneous intrusion; life is a closed book, or a well-rehearsed play.

Enter the child. His mind has not yet been closed to the unexpected, his vision of hope not yet obstructed by the pessimistic dogmas of cultural realism. He has the courage to see—and believe—at least until the forms of repression become dominant. He is the trusting person and is therefore open to receive Jesus and the Kingdom:

> Let the children come to me . . . for to such belongs the kingdom of

God. Truly, I say to you, whoever does not receive the kingdom of God like a child shall not enter it (Mark 10:14, 15).

Second, children are models of *humility*. The adult world is preoccupied with status, some types of which are 'earned' and others types of which are inherited. Status is the measurement of self-worth in terms of comparisons with those whom the social system deems above or below us. Jesus introduced a Kingdom of only one status: child of God. That is why we must all 'turn and become like children' if we are to enter it. That is why there are no status claims to be made. That is why membership demands humility (see Matthew 18:1-4).

Humility is the gift of honesty about oneself. Adult culture conditions us to mould ourselves into images that conform to the present world order. The Kingdom eliminates artificial image and presumptuous status, and invites the faithful to become children and accept themselves. Except we become as children, we cannot know who we are.

Third, children are models for *helping us to understand God and his ways*. The adult 'realist' accepts the world as it is and accommodates himself to it. He understands as he has been taught to understand; what he knows is what he needs to know in order to function in the social system. Imagination is dysfunctional. The child, on the other hand, has not been sufficiently socialised to impose thought structures and dogmatisms upon his perception of the world. Rather, he is open to ideas and possibilities which simply seem to be right or beautiful. He is open to revelation from outside cultural imposition.

The Christian faith is based upon revelation. It says that God speaks for himself through means that he chooses and that his word comes to those who are willing to see, hear and touch that which transcends the perspectives, dogmas and 'realities' of the present world order. The word of God comes to those who are ready to shed the securities of personal and cultural idolatry, in this sense to become unlearned again, and to open themselves to divine invasion. To become impressionable before God: children.

At that time Jesus declared, 'I thank thee, Father, Lord of heaven and earth, that thou hast hidden these things from the wise and understanding and revealed them to babes . . .' (Matthew 11:25).

Clearly, children have important things to teach the Church[100] and through their more untarnished sight may give it a clearer and more courageous vision of God's future. Hence, churches that treat children condescendingly as empty vessels of humanity which are to be filled with adult 'reality' are missing the mark. They are rejecting gifts of God and closing their fellowship to important spokespersons.[101] The Church of the future loves children and learns from them.

It is worth noting here that the early Salvationist movement emphasised the ability of children to respond to the gospel and organised young converts and the children of senior soldiers into youth corps. The child, in other words, could become a participant in the life and ministry of the corps fellowship; he could become a junior soldier. To be sure, the education of junior soldiers reflected mostly the views of adults about Christian life, but there was strong conviction about the ability of children to experience God and receive the Kingdom.

In a rather amazing book published in 1884, William Booth expounded his views on raising children. Many of the views are thoroughly Victorian, but there are nevertheless some radical statements having to do with the divine potentiality of children. For example, Booth cautions parents against the danger of presenting the faith to their children as a matter of the understanding (adult theology) and of using their own experiences of God as the standard for the young.[102] To objections to his allowing children to speak and pray publicly, he answers that he is not too concerned about the theological 'errors' they may make since true Christianity is more a matter of the heart and conscience than of the intellect.[103] All this points to an understanding of Christian experience as primarily a matter of God at work in the heart and through spiritual intuition, and therefore at work in the lives of all who are open to his influence—whether adults or children. It points to a fellowship in which the place and participation of children are treasured. The children, no less than the adults, can lead the Church into the future.

We have described three important ways in which the future toward which the Church is moving moulds the character of the fellowship of believers and overcomes barriers to its shared life. Other ways could also have been identified and developed, but the three we have treated are among the most crucial and can serve as models.

(c) The future in mission

In chapter 4 we developed the concept of the Church as a

missionary army. We shall now consider how the future toward which the Church is moving determines how the Church's mission is carried out and the battles fought. As a colony of hope in a despairing world, the Church moves forward in mission with *urgency, patience* and *optimism.*

The proclamation of the gospel in the New Testament always carries a note of *urgency.* The Church lives between the two advents of its Lord and must therefore live in anticipation and evangelise with compulsion. Our Lord makes clear that the time before the second advent cannot be presumed upon:

> But of that day or that hour no one knows, not even the angels in heaven, nor the Son, but only the Father. Take heed, watch; for you do not know when the time will come (Mark 13:32, 33).

The apostle Paul urges his Corinthian readers not to take their salvation lightly, but rather to accept the full implications of it *now*:

> Behold, now is the acceptable time; behold, now is the day of salvation (2 Corinthians 6:2).

In his letter to the Romans, he says it is time to wake from sleep and be aware that (final) salvation is getting nearer and nearer, and he admonishes his readers to cast off the works of darkness and live in the daylight of the Kingdom—that is, to 'put on the Lord Jesus Christ' (Romans 13:11-14).

The Church of the future therefore implements its mission with an awareness of the nearness of the Kingdom's consummation. This is not to say that its evangelism uses the 'panic' method, urging people to be saved today because terrible wrath is just around the corner. The urgency of the gospel is not a manipulative tool; it is the announcement of the fact that the Kingdom that came in Jesus is moving toward realisation in the plan of God, and that this reality invites response. Nor does this awareness result in social involvement that is superficial, shallow or nonexistent. The urgency of the gospel is not an excuse from social action for the reason of obsessive evangelism. Rather, social action is the necessary complement to evangelism, demonstrates the emerging power of the gospel in the world, and thereby reinforces the reality of the coming Kingdom. The urgency of the Church's mission is expressed in the seriousness and depth of both its evangelism and its social action.

Hence, the Church also moves forward with *patience.* There is no call for it to proceed with 'quick fixes', nor is there reason to hurry results. Urgency is not impatience. The call to battle *is* urgent, but the battles must be carefully planned and prepared for. The timing must be right, or the victory will not be sure. The missionary Church moves decisively, but also patiently.

The New Testament provides two analogies that reveal the importance of waiting in mission. One is a tree or plant bearing fruit, the other is salt being applied to food.

Jesus once told this parable:

> The kingdom of God is as if a man should scatter seed upon the ground, and should sleep and rise night and day, and the seed should sprout and grow, he knows not how. The earth produces of itself, first the blade, then the ear, then the full grain in the ear. But when the grain is ripe, at once he puts in the sickle, because the harvest has come (Mark 4:26-29).

There is an unfolding, a natural timing in the Kingdom's manifestation in human life. The Kingdom is a seed that grows gradually into maturity (Matthew 13:31, 32), a lump of leaven that slowly brings its influence to bear in the chosen loaf (13:13), the fruit that ripens in time on a healthy tree (7:17). As a sign of the unfolding Kingdom, fruitfulness is a mark of Christ's abiding presence in the Church and of the Church abiding in him (John 15:1-8).

Fruitfulness is not productivity. It is the natural outcome of the Christ life. It is not forcing results. It is allowing the seeds of mission to sprout, grow and bear fruit. Productivity distrusts the future, and therefore attempts to force it. Fruitfulness trusts the future, invests in it, lives by it and waits patiently for it. It is the only means by which the Church moves forward in mission.

The other analogy of the Church's patience in mission is that of salt being scattered on food. Jesus called his followers 'the salt of the earth' (Matthew 5:13). They were to preserve and they were to season. Both functions emphasised process rather than productivity. As a preservative, salt kept food from spoiling; in a similar way, the Church is present in the world to keep it from spoiling, from losing the Kingdom and failing to move toward God's future. As a seasoning, salt was used to enhance the food's flavour and stimulate the appetite; and in like manner, the Church sprinkles itself into the world, giving a flavour of the Kingdom and an invitation to the future.

It is the mission of the Church to plant the Kingdom like seeds and to be scattered like salt. The wise farmer allows the needed time for proper cultivation and fruition; the experienced cook uses only the right amount of salt. There is a timing and even a certain restraint in the Kingdom's unfolding. The mission of the Church is not an independent venture; it is a witness, in word and deed, to the Kingdom implanted by Jesus Christ, and it is a sensitive cultivation of its growth in fertile soil. The missionary Church sows urgently, and waits patiently.

The missionary Church also moves forward with *optimism*. Warning his disciples that they would be scarred and scattered by tribulation, Jesus follows with: '. . . but be of good cheer, I have overcome the world' (John 16:33). Here is Jesus claiming victory even *before* the victory! Unrestrained by time's blocked vision of tomorrow, victory was secure in the mind of God and in the heart of his Christ. It is with firm confidence that Jesus says, 'Now is the judgment of this world, now shall the ruler of this world be cast out . . .' (John 12:31). It is with equal confidence that he acknowledges in prayer that the Father '. . . hast given [the Son] power over all flesh, to give eternal life to all whom [the Father] has given him' (John 17:2). The cross is to complete, and the resurrection seal, the victory already given.

This is the best possible news for the world. It is the evangelical basis for optimism, which is belief in the best. The question for the Church, as it moves forward in mission, is: do you believe? Our Lord's victory is shared with those who *believe* in it and are willing to take the risks to which this confidence always leads. It is not surprising, then, that John links the believer's faith in Jesus as the Son of God with 'the victory that overcomes the world' (1 John 5:4, 5). The missionary Church moves forward in the confidence of Jesus' victory, and only in this confidence can it effectively give witness to and facilitate the Kingdom's triumph.

The Church is therefore to be understood as an eschatological community that engages in mission in response to God's future. In Jesus Christ God gives the possibility of the future (the consummation of the Kingdom) to those who are open. The mission of the Church is to urge persons to be receptive to this reality, to be patient with the processes by which the Kingdom comes to fruition in the lives of persons and communities, and to believe fervently and actively in the victorious outcome of God's action in the world. Only in this way is the Church truly God's eschatological community.

(d) The future in structure

In dominating the structure[104] of the Church, God's future calls for a missionary pragmatism that continually reshapes that structure in preparation for the Kingdom's coming. In fact, ecclesiastical structures are truly evangelical when, and to the extent that, they open fellowship and ministry to the future. When structures obstruct movement toward God's future in Christ, when they constrict openness to the coming, transforming Kingdom, they are ready to be changed for the sake of the gospel. A missionary ecclesiology sees such change as a natural, healthy process in the Church's movement toward the future. Sometimes the change must be radical. Whatever steps need to be taken *must* be taken. The eschatological community is willing, if necessary, to be institutionally abolished.

Consider the attitude of Jesus toward ecclesiastical structures. He was not an iconoclast who gloated over the demise of people's traditions and institutions. As a devout Jew, he came to uphold and fulfil the law and the prophets (Matthew 5:17-20). He affirmed the reason for which they came into being: to point to and prepare for the *Kingdom* (Matthew 22:34-40; Luke 6:27-36; cf Galatians 5:14; Romans 13:8-10). But he also understood that traditions could outlive their usefulness in God's purposes and that structures that once served those purposes well could actually become hindrances to the emerging Kingdom. After his heart-rending lament over apostate Jerusalem, his disciples gestured toward the buildings of the Temple. No doubt they feared what he might say about the future of this focal point of their Jewish faith. They had good reason. He said:

> Truly, I say to you, there will not be left here one stone upon another, that will not be thrown down (Matthew 24:2).

The Kingdom had come in Jesus. The Temple could no longer be a spiritual focal point. Worship could no longer focus on this place; it must now focus on his Person. The Temple would crumble; they were to let it crumble for themselves. What had become obsolete must now be abandoned.

As the eschatological community that is committed to the future, the Church is a people who are free to abandon structures that no longer hold promise for helping them to move decisively toward that future. When a decision-making process is so cumbersome as to create missionary inertia and so ingrown as to create self-serving goals, it should be abandoned. When the processes and procedures of ecclesiastical government block forward movement, they should be abandoned. When traditional programmes that were once effective for the cause of Christ become stale and lifeless, they should be abandoned. When rituals lose their ability to evoke the meaning of the gospel and to challenge participants to respond to God's call, they should be abandoned.

What *then?* How are new structures found that will better nurture the spiritual growth and further the Church's mission in the world? The answer is given to God's people when they prayerfully seek the wisdom and courage to structure their ecclesiastical building so as to make a home for the future in Christ. The answer is given to a Luther, a Wesley, a Booth or any disciple of Christ who is interested only in structures that are open to the future, that invite the Kingdom into the fellowship, that facilitate the pilgrimage, that serve the mission. The answer is given to those who allow the future to dominate structure. It will sometimes mean the abandonment of a structure that cannot nurture the future, and replacement with a new one. Other times it will mean the renewal and revision of structures that have become too inert. Still other times it will mean the affirmation and strengthening of existing structures that effectively move the Church towards the future in Christ. In each case the process is the same: building the structure that for now and in this setting best opens up the possibilities for persons to receive the Kingdom and to become fellow citizens with the saints and members of

> the household of God, built upon the foundation of the apostles and prophets, Christ Jesus himself being the cornerstone, in whom the whole structure is joined together and grows into a holy temple in the Lord . . . (Ephesians 2:19-21).

Eschatological celebration and renewal: feasting on the future

We have defined the Church eschatologically as the colony of hope that prays for the coming Kingdom and lives in the light of its dawning. We have developed this character in terms of how the Church lives its life and carries out its mission. In concluding this chapter we must now speak of the ways in which the Church enhances this understanding through celebrations and rituals, how it drives the point home and keeps awareness keen. We must now speak of the *feasts of the future.*

All *worship* is a feast of the future. The music of worship lifts the congregation not out of the world but into the future of the world; as the language of the sublime, it opens worshippers to a future that is beyond the vision of the present world order. The words of hymns bring the vision into focus. Corporate prayer unites worshippers in gratitude for the future which the saving work of Jesus Christ makes possible and in petition for the coming of the Kingdom in fullness. The reading and preaching of the Scriptures are both an exposition of what God has done for mankind and an expectation of its consummation in the world, in the Church and in the life of each hearer. Special celebrations in worship services are opportunities to mark the ways in which the Church, and specifically the local congregation, are receiving the Kingdom and moving forward toward the future of its realisation.[105] Acts of response—including the giving of tithes and offerings, affirmations or confessions of faith, moving forward to a place of prayer, and in some traditions confessions of sin, are specific expressions of how the people of God can free themselves from enslavement and open themselves to the future which God has given in Christ. Christian worship is a feast of the future.

But there are specific celebrations that especially evoke the eschatological reality of the Church. These are: baptism, soldier enrolment, the Lord's supper, the love feast and foot washing.

As we have seen (chapters 3 and 4), *baptism* in the early Church was more a celebration of the commencement of Christian pilgrimage, of the joining of the pilgrim band, of the enlistment in battle as a soldier of Jesus Christ, than it was a conferring of spiritual status. Understood in this way, baptism can be an eschatological celebration that evokes the reality not only of the new birth in Christ but also of the new future in Christ. In baptism the believer catches a vision of what he will become, what the Church will become, and what the world will become. Properly understood, baptism is initiation into the future.

Soldier enrolment in Salvationist tradition is also an initiation into the future. Here the oath is taken to obey Jesus Christ as Commander-in-Chief and to devote one's life 'to his service for the salvation of the world'. The focus is the future, and the commitment being made is to the inevitable triumph of God's redemptive plan for the world. The soldier being enrolled is not receiving privileges; he is being commissioned to fight battles. The character of those battles is determined by the future because the eschatological Church claims that the future is the Kingdom's realisation and then bases its life and mission on that claim. This posture brings it into conflict with a world that sees a different future, or none at all. Soldier enrolment is a baptism for battle carried out against the background of the Kingdom's inevitable triumph.

The *Lord's supper* is also celebrated against the background of the Kingdom's anticipated realisation. It is a feast partaken of both in remembrance of the Lord and in expectation of his return (1 Corinthians 11:24, 26). The *love feast* emphasises the fellowship dimension of this eschatological character. The community of faith anticipates the coming Kingdom by claiming Christ's reconciliation in their life together. The love feast is a celebration of this reconciliation, whether the feast be a ritual meal or an actual meal together in which the unifying presence of the Lord is recognised. As such, it, along with the Lord's supper, evokes the future and provokes the Church to risk receiving it.

Foot washing is an example of a ritual that provokes awareness of how the future is to be received. It is a celebration of servanthood as the form of Christ's reconciling mission to the world and as the way in which the Kingdom becomes concrete reality in the fellowship of believers. As our Lord was among us as one who served, so are we with one another as servants (Luke 22:24-27). As servants we anticipate the future in which Christ's lordship is realised in service to him and to those whom he loves. In service (servanthood in action), therefore, the Church moves decisively toward the future. Foot washing is an affirmation of this future and a denial of the self-aggrandisement of the past.

But the Church is called not only to the service of members toward one another, but also to service in and for the world. The mission of the Church in the world is the servant people of God actively moving forward to the future of the world by giving themselves. They give themselves wherever their service can bring liberation and wholeness and thus witness to the coming Kingdom. In doing so they perform what has been called *the sacrament of the good Samaritan.* This is the sacrament of the Church in mission, the sacrament in which the healing, reconciling grace of God becomes incarnate as a servant dresses the wounds of one who is otherwise looked upon as an enemy. It is an open sign of the radical transformation of personal and social relationships in the light of the Kingdom's future. It is both a feat and a feast: it calls for courageous, self-sacrificing action, and it actually imbibes the new life in Christ. It is a living invitation to the world to partake of the Kingdom feast and discover the joys of servanthood. It is an opening to the future.

But nowhere is the Church more open to the future than in *prayer*. In prayer the Church bows its head before God so that it can lift its vision to the future which he graciously gives. Prayer is the Church then asking God:

> Thy kingdom come,
> Thy will be done,
> On earth as it is in heaven (Matthew 6:10).

Prayer is the Church hearing its Lord promise, 'Surely I am coming soon,' and answering, 'Amen. Come, Lord Jesus!' (Revelation 22:20). Prayer is the Church preparing itself to receive the Kingdom and to live in the light of its dawning. Prayer is the Church opening itself to the future.

Epilogue

THIS work now draws to a close. It will have failed to achieve its purpose, however, if the reader goes no further in attempting to formulate and re-formulate his understanding of the Church. We hope that the non-Salvationist reader has been given a better view of Salvationist ecclesiology and possibly helped in the development of his own. We hope that the Salvationist reader has been stimulated to rethink his own conceptions of the Army's place in the Church and its mission in the world.

The Army began as an evangelistic agency with no intention of becoming a church. Hence, its eleven doctrinal articles included no ecclesiological statements. The omission has not been felt keenly until recent years. Now, many within the movement feel the need to develop an ecclesiological understanding that will enable Salvationists better to understand the nature and calling of the Church, the peculiar calling of the Army as a branch of the Church, and the contribution of the Army to the Church. This work is only one step in that direction.

No Salvationist need consider himself a stepchild of the Church; nor are there grounds for claiming Salvationist superiority. The Salvation Army is a legitimate part of the Church, neither above it nor below it. What it is and does has no validity outside the gospel that calls the Church into being. Its mandate for mission is the Church's mandate. The Church's calling is the Army's calling. Bramwell Booth put it this way, and with this we conclude:

> We believe that our Lord Jesus Christ has called us into his Church of the redeemed, that our call has not been by man or the will of man, but by the Holy Spirit of God; that our salvation is from him, not by ceremonies or sacraments or ordinances of this period or that, but by the pardoning life-giving work of our divine Saviour. We believe also that our system for extending the knowledge and power of his gospel, and of nurturing and governing the believing people gathered into our ranks, is as truly and fully in harmony with the

spirit set forth and the principles laid down by Jesus Christ and his apostles as those which have been adopted by our brethren of other times or of other folds.[106]

Amen.

Religious Doctrines of The Salvation Army

1 We believe that the Scriptures of the Old and New Testaments were given by inspiration of God, and that they only constitute the Divine rule of Christian faith and practice.

2 We believe that there is only one God, who is infinitely perfect, the Creator, Preserver, and Governor of all things, and who is the only proper object of religious worship.

3 We believe that there are three persons in the Godhead—the Father, the Son and the Holy Ghost, individed in essence and co-equal in power and glory.

4 We believe that in the person of Jesus Christ the Divine and human natures are united, so that He is truly and properly God and truly and properly man.

5 We believe that our first parents were created in a state of innocency, but by their disobedience they lost their purity and happiness, and that in consequence of their fall all men have become sinners, totally depraved, and as such are justly exposed to the wrath of God.

6 We believe that the Lord Jesus Christ has by His suffering and death made an atonement for the whole world so that whosoever will may be saved.

7 We believe that repentance towards God, faith in our Lord Jesus Christ, and regeneration by the Holy Spirit, are necessary to salvation.

8 We believe that we are justified by grace through faith in our Lord Jesus Christ and that he that believeth hath the witness in himself.

9 We believe that continuance in a state of salvation depends upon continued obedient faith in Christ.

10 We believe that it is the privilege of all believers to be wholly sanctified, and that their whole spirit and soul and body may be preserved blameless unto the coming of our Lord Jesus Christ.

11 We believe in the immortality of the soul; in the resurrection of the body; in the general judgment at the end of the world; in the eternal happiness of the righteous; and in the endless punishment of the wicked.

Salvation Army Act 1980

Notes

1

In this study the term 'ecclesiology' is used to refer to a theology of the Church, or doctrines of the nature, purpose and mission of the Church that together constitute a comprehensive theology of the Church.

2

'Essential' here means that each of the six realities is necessary to the whole. Without any one of them, the Church cannot be the Church.

3

The word 'obedience' here is used not in the sense of slavish adherence to rules or abdication of personal initiative and responsibility, but rather as the action corollary of faith in Jesus as Lord. Such faith *leads* to obedience. The paradox of *this* obedience is that it is the way to freedom.

4

We shall not here focus on the issue of infant versus believers' baptism. From a Salvationist perspective, the major issues are twofold: first, the nature of 'sacraments' in Christian faith and practice and, second, the extent to which a sacrament like baptism is considered important or even necessary in the life of the believer.

5

See *Baptism, Eucharist and Ministry,* World Council of Churches, 1982, pp 2-6.

6

Adopting a prevailing custom because of its symbolic potential in that cultural situation is one thing. Elevating that choice to the claim of initiating a rite which *must* be observed in every era and cultural context is quite another. Furthermore, insisting as some fellowships do that the rite of water baptism, properly administered, conveys saving grace *of itself* does violence to the New Testament meaning of conversion as a life changing event between a person and God through

Jesus Christ in the power of the Holy Spirit *without* any requirement of ecclesiastical or institutional administration. Such insistence leads naturally to the practice of infant baptism: if saving grace can be received automatically as the result of a properly administered rite, then infants can somehow undergo a spiritual rebirth through water baptism. Such a view, while usually focusing on the faith of the one administering the rite, the parents and the fellowship as effectual on behalf of the infant, ignores any necessity of faith on the part of the recipient and thereby undermines the New Testament understanding of faith as personal response to Jesus Christ, a response that cannot be made on behalf of someone else. It is our view that the integrity of the Church is undermined when incorporation of members into the Body—in the true spiritual meaning of that phrase—is not a conscious act of faith on the part of each person.

John the Baptist adopted a customary mode of initiation but also stated that water baptism would be superseded by baptism with the Holy Spirit in the messianic ministry (Mark 1:8). John the Evangelist pointed out that while our Lord's disciples baptised, Jesus himself did not (John 4:2). The resurrected Jesus announced to his disciples that whereas John had baptised with water, *they* would be baptised with the Holy Spirit (Acts 1:5). The apostle Paul disparaged the place and necessity of water baptism in his own ministry (1 Corinthians 1:14-17). None of this evidence undermines the practice of water baptism as a potentially helpful and poignant symbolic rite testifying to true conversion. It does, however, call into question the claims both of a necessary connection between water and Spirit baptism and of the elevation of the rite itself to spiritual efficaciousness.

7

Traditionally, the new soldier dons his Salvation Army *uniform* for the first time when enrolled. Although the uniform is not worn by all soldiers today, it is a strong symbol of the transformation which conversion effects and the disciplined life to which all Christians are called. It represents the change wrought, the reclothing in Christ, and the call to battle against principalities and powers.

8

We wish to note here that none of the doctrinal statements which follows is unique to Salvationist theology. We contend that they are scripturally based and indispensable for an adequate ecclesiology.

9

John Coutts argues convincingly that the real significance of the Army's nonsacramental position, the real issue being fought over, is 'the immediacy of grace'. ('The Army's Contribution to the Churches', *The Officer,* September 1965, Volume XVI, No 9, pp 601, 602.)

10
This unity does not, of course, exclude diversity. The diversity of God's people can be mutually enriching and productive precisely *because* of the unity in faith and obedience.

11
Some early Salvationists were so intent upon disparaging the efficacy of sacraments alone that they argued themselves almost to the brink of a Gnostic anti-materialism. Both Catherine Booth and George Scott Railton wanted the elimination of rituals as dangerous temptations to reliance upon the physical and avoidance of authentic divine experience. Bramwell Booth remembered that Railton argued

> in favour of abandoning all ceremonials which were prominently associated with the rest of the religious life of the world . . . he claimed that the freedom which was purchased by Jesus Christ was a freedom from all that belonged to the old dispensation, including the whole ceremonial principle (Bramwell Booth, 'Sacraments', *The Staff Review,* January 1923, No 5, p 54).

The Salvation Army, of course, did not eliminate the ritual element. It developed new rituals in keeping with its unique character and mission. These rituals can be as much abused and trivialised as any other. The only way to keep this from happening is to celebrate them as signs of and witnesses to the independent gracious work of God in the life of the world of the believer. Herein lies the true Salvationist understanding of ritual.

12
There are a remarkable number of words in the New Testament having the prefix *syn-* ('with'), which describe how Christians participate with one another and stand alongside one another in varying circumstances of life and Christian endeavour: prisoner-with, servant-with, worker-with, citizen-with, soldier-with, passionate-with, suffering-with, rejoice-with, labour-with, fighting shoulder to shoulder-with, finding rest together-with, building-with, comforting-with, heir-with, members of the body-with, partakers-with, etc.

13
Even the later council in Jerusalem (Acts 15) did not seem to be highly formalised in structure, and the decisions that were made were what '. . . seemed good to the apostles and the elders, *with the whole church* . . .' (15:22).

14
This aspect of the Church's calling is dealt with in chapter 4.

15
Sociologist Robert Nesbit has asserted that in the 20th century 'alienated man' is the key figure of thought and the quest for community is the most impressive fact (*The Quest for Community,* London: Oxford University Press, 1953, pp vii, 10).

16
The War Cry (London, 17 January 1883).

17
The Song Book of The Salvation Army (1986 edition), Song No 7, verse 4.

18
Athenagoras, *A Plea Regarding Christians,* ed and trans Cyril C. Richardson, *Early Christian Fathers,* The Library of Christian Classics, vol 1 (Philadelphia: The Westminster Press, 1953), p 310.

19
If the reader requires proof of this statement, there are numerous writings which convincingly show that there is insufficient evidence to support the claim that Jesus actually intended to institute the supper as a sacrament. Emil Brunner (*The Christian Doctrine of the Church, Faith, and the Consummation,* Dogmatics: vol III, trans David Cairns, Philadelphia: The Westminster Press, 1962, pp 60ff) shows that the development of the Lord's supper as a sacrament was an outcome of the growing influence of the sacramental view of salvation and the progressive institutionalisation of the Church in its early centuries. Vernard Eller says bluntly:

> 'Sacraments' do not fit the historical context of original Christianity; neither do they fit the theological context. Sacraments constitute about as 'religious' a technique as can be devised; and original Christianity was religionless (*In Place of Sacraments:* A study of baptism and the Lord's supper, Grand Rapids: W. B. Eerdmans Pub Co, 1972, p 12).

Salvationist writers have written able defences of The Salvation Army's nonsacramental position and in doing so have demonstrated the lack of a scholarly basis for asserting that Jesus instituted the supper as a sacrament. Here are some of their works:

> *The Sacraments, the Salvationist's Viewpoint* (London: Salvationist Publishing and Supplies, 1960).
>
> William Metcalf, *The Salvationist and the Sacraments* (London: SP & S, 1965).

Clifford W. Kew, *Closer Communion* (London: SP & S, 1980).

Commissioner Francis W. Pearce, 'The Lord's Supper', *The Officer,* March 1923, pp 213-217.

'The Attitude of The Salvation Army toward the Sacraments', manuscript anonymous, the Salvation Army's New York Archives, *circa* 1910, pp 27.

20
The presumed 'words of institution' of Jesus which the apostle Paul records (1 Corinthians 11:23-26) emphasise Jesus' desire that his followers remember this event but do not require that this be done through sacramental ritual. On the contrary, it seems that the Corinthian church met regularly for fellowship meals but that these frequently degenerated into selfish indulgences and factional disputes. Paul quotes Jesus' words in order to remind them that these meals together were a communion with their Lord and through him with one another. They had forgotten. Hence, the significance of Jesus' words that *whenever* his followers share a meal together, they are to remember him and worthily celebrate the new community of love which his sacrifice made possible.

21
Brunner, p 63.

22
It is worth noting that in an article written after the decision to discontinue observance of the sacraments, William Booth asks this rhetorical question: '. . . is it not wise for us to postpone any settlement of the question, to leave it over to some future day, when we shall have more light, and see more clearly our way before us?' (*The War Cry,* London, 17 January 1883). The door was not completely closed; the Army was not opposed to the sacraments.

23
Bramwell Booth, *Echoes and Memories* (New York: George H. Doran, 1925).

24
See footnote 11.

25
Let it be noted that the issue of observance or non-observance of the sacraments in the Army today must be engaged on the basis of

theological concerns and scriptural interpretation, not the practical problems of the early years, almost all of which no longer exist.

26
M. H. Shepherd, Jr, 'The Lord's Supper', *The Interpreter's Dictionary of the Bible* (New York: Abingdon Press, 1962), vol III, pp 158, 159.

27
Eller, p 39.

28
Ibid, p 86.

29
'Love Feasts: An aid to Harmony in the Corps', *The Officer*, September 1923, pp 194-196.

30
It should be pointed out that most corps officers are married couples. Hence, in the 'serving' of the meal, a meal setting more akin to the home setting is evoked. Furthermore, since single women officers comprise another smaller but sizeable percentage of corps officers, the female participation is considerable, a fact which closely corresponds to the mother's role at meal times in two-parent and most single-parent (female-headed) families.

31
This writer has never participated in a love feast in which he has not perceived the Kingdom in a way that brought exhilaration, experienced the oneness of the fellowship as an indisputable reality, sensed that healing was taking place at the time, and departed with greater resolve and empowerment to be an agent of reconciliation. It is to be hoped that the Army of the future will claim this worthy celebration of its early years as an observance which has the potential for nurturing love and mutual support within the body.

32
Bramwell Booth, 'Sacraments', *The Staff Review,* January 1923, No 5, p 55.

33
Bramwell Booth, *Echoes,* p 155.

34
Ibid, p 69.

35
Augustine (*ca* 400) first attested the ceremonial washing of the feet in church liturgy in connection with the Easter baptisms in certain churches a foot-washing ceremony on Maundy Thursday is in the seventh-century liturgy of the church in Spain, and the custom has continued in some churches to the present day. Shepherd, 'Foot Washing', *The Interpreter's Dictionary of the Bible* (NY: Abingdon Press, 1962), vol II, p 308.

36
Ibid.

37
As of the date of this writing, the author has been a participant in two foot washings, one led by an Episcopal priest, the other led by a Salvation Army officer. On both occasions the feelings and perceptions described in the text were present in a quiet but exhilarating way.

38
We are not saying that social rootlessness guarantees openness to spiritual change, nor are we suggesting that persons who have strong social roots and are well integrated into a stable social environment are not open to such change. Rather, we are pointing out that, on the whole, spiritual revolutions and reformations seem to have most frequently occurred among those groups who have a minimal or decreasing personal investment in social orders which fabricate spiritual and political idolatries. Examples would be: the Old Testament prophets who threw ecclesiastical advancement and social acceptance to the wind by exposing the godless immorality of a civilised Hebrew nation; the slaves and politically powerless peoples of the first- and second-century Roman Empire, among whom Christianity had its most extensive appeal; the mendicant friars of the Middle Ages who abandoned the security of settled religious life for the drifter lifestyle of roving preachers; the less privileged classes of 18th-century England, who made the most substantial response in the great Wesleyan revival.

39
George W. Webber, *The Congregation in Mission* (New York: Abingdon Press, 1964), p 120.

40
Eller, pp 26ff.

41
Ibid, pp 30ff.

42
The Salvation Army flag consists of three colours: *red*, symbolising God's redemptive work in Christ and therefore the saving grace which has transformed the Salvationist's life; *blue*, symbolising God's purity and also the purity which marks the lives of those who single-mindedly pursue discipleship; and *yellow* (in the shape of a blazing star), symbolising the cleansing and empowering fire of the Holy Spirit by which discipleship becomes possible.

43
See, eg, Eller, pp 32-35.

44
For example, the prominence of elders (*presbuteroi*) in the Judean Church demonstrates the continuance of the Jewish model of religious government, a model that was very suitable for both organisation and mission in the Jewish milieu. As the Church moved westward, it increasingly adopted an episcopal form of government which corresponded to Roman organisation and provided a means of authoritative guidance, teaching and assignment which the rapidly growing movement required in Gentile soil.

45
Harvey Cox, *God's Revolution and Man's Responsibility* (Valley Forge: The Judson Press, 1965), pp 115ff. Cox notes: the apostle Paul's use of the soldier's armour as an analogy of the resources and protection needed by the Christian in his life in the world; the New Testament use of the word *paganus,* meaning one who was not in military service, to refer to those who were not the people of God; and the designation of Jesus as *kurios,* the commander, the one who was to be obeyed in political and military decisions. Cox also concedes that the military terminology has some dangers when adopted uncritically and that the limits of its application to the life of the Church should be spelled out. He specifically mentions two of these dangers. First, armies tend to develop rank systems which create a military élite who control the decision making and wield power over the common soldiers. This is precisely what happened in the evolution of an early Church hierarchy. Second, armies tend to shed blood; they are organised to attack an outside enemy. Cox points out that the soldier of Christ fights for *shalom,* that '. . . the difference between him and a soldier of Caesar is that, instead of shedding someone else's blood, he sheds his own. He pours himself out as a sacrifice. He dies in order to win. His victory is his defeat' (p 117).

46
Hans-Ruedi Weber, *Salty Christians* (New York: Seabury Press, 1963), p 25.

47
Chapter 5 will deal with the important nurturing role of small groups in the Church.

48
George W. Webber, p 179.

49
Robert S. Paul, *The Church in Search of Its Self* (Grand Rapids: Erdmans, 1972), p 123.

50
Ibid, pp 141, 142.

51
Ibid. p 153.

52
Paul cautions against three dangers of a pragmatic approach to Church order. The first is the danger of *creating a spurious tradition.* Traditions which were originally evangelically pragmatic often become self-perpetuating and assume a false aura of sanctity; they become institutionalised as standard operating procedures. These, in turn, become obstacles to change, especially since they often *speak* of mission. The only way to avoid this tendency is the continued practice of evangelical pragmatism in re-ordering the life of the Church.

The second danger is that of a particular congregation or denomination *mistaking the gospel's objectives for its own.* A congregation may falsely assume that the gospel is at the centre of its plans and that its orders are coming from Jesus Christ. It may even identify its own prosperity with the expansion of God's Kingdom. The antidote, of course, is critical self-evaluation as a part of continuing evangelical pragmatism. The Church's mission requires ongoing institutional change in response to God's activity in the world terrain, and the only way in which the Church can be faithful to its missionary calling is to *continue* pragmatic adaptation of methods and structures to the needs of the gospel in each new situation. Obsolete forms would be shed, and new forms which facilitate missionary responsiveness in the present context would be adopted.

The third danger is that of *'selling out'.* The facility for pragmatic adaptation is transferred from application to the needs of the gospel to application to personal or institutional ends. The transfer can be very subtle, and therefore insidious. An institution's objectives become closely identified with the cause of the gospel, and attempts at self-aggrandisement within the institution, or on the part of the institution, are so cloaked in evangelical piety that identification of real motives becomes difficult. Religious institutions can be perfect cover-ups for opportunism.

What the missionary Church needs constantly to keep before itself is the need for an *evangelical* pragmatism—that is, a pragmatism that serves only the *gospel.* The Church is called to be pragmatic *for the gospel's sake*! Pragmatic decisions, therefore, must always be made in the context of asking what the gospel in the world requires. (*Ibid,* pp 158-160.)

53
Quoted in *The Officer,* February 1983, p 70.

54
William Booth, 'The Future of Missions, and the Mission of the Future', *The War Cry,* 8 June 1889.

55
Catherine Booth, *The Salvation Army in relation to the Church and State, and other addresses* (London: The Salvation Army Publishing Dept, 1883), p 29.

56
It should also be pointed out, however, that there was a serious omission made because the movement came into being as an evangelistic agency with no intention of becoming a church fellowship (denomination) as well. There is no stated doctrine of the Church.

57
Charles M. Olsen, 'Small Groups: One way to renewal', *Church in Mission* (Presbyterian Church in the United States, July 1969), pp 9, 10.

58
'Kingdom' is basically a socio-political concept. The Kingdom of God as understood by Jesus is a socio-political reality in which God rules (*basileia* = rule, reign), every citizen has infinite worth (see, eg, Matthew 11:11), love is the source of power in *all* relationships (see, eg, Matthew 5:43-48), and the priorities of a power-hungry world are reversed (see, eg, Mark 10:17-31).

59
Jesus radically personalised the concept of the Kingdom. He spoke of it in terms of a person's realtionship to the Father; he called for individual repentance (see Mark 1:15) and belief in himself (see especially John's gospel 3:16, 18, 36; 6:35, 47; 9:35; 12:46; 14:1), he identified the gospel with his own person (see Mark 8:35). All of this points to the necessity of personal response to, and relationships with, the one in whom the Kingdom is realised. The Kingdom is through Jesus alone (see John 14:6). Hence personal invitation to confront Jesus as Lord is essential to the Church's missionary witness.

60
Quoted by Brigadier Fred Fox, lecture to cadets, 4 January 1924, The Salvation Army Archives, New York.

61
Quoted from the articles of war in use, 1987.

62
William Booth, *International Social Council Addresses, 1911* (London: The Salvation Army Printing Works, 1912), pp 63ff.

63
W. T. Stead, *General Booth, A Biographical Sketch* (London: Isbister and Co, Ltd, 1891), p 68.

64
The Christian Mission Magazine, September 1878.

65
See, for example, K. S. Inglis, *Churches and the Working Classes in Victorian England* (London: Routledge and Kegan Paul, 1963).

66
Accounts of major defections and splits during the first thirty years of the movement's history provide interesting corroboration of the importance of unity and autocracy in building the Army's missionary strength. For the most part, these groups that parted company died out rather quickly. The one exception worth mentioning, the Volunteers of America, itself developed an autocratic, unified government.

67
An important distinction between *adaptation* and *identification* needs to be made. Adaptation is suiting of missionary language, forms, concerns and methods to the social and cultural situation of the people targeted in

mission. Identification, as we have used the term in this book, refers to a 'sellout' to the prevailing culture, the uncritical adoption of its values (whether overtly or covertly), and the consequent role played by churches to 'sacralise' the values of that culture rather than those of the new Kingdom in Christ.

68
Quoted in St John Ervine, *God's Soldier: General William Booth* (New York: The Macmillan Co, 1935), p 390.

69
William Booth, *The Doctrines and Disciplines of The Salvation Army* (London: International Headquarters of The Salvation Army, 1881), p 41.

70
Robert Sandall, *The History of The Salvation Army* (London: Thomas Nelson and Sons Ltd, 3 vols), vol 2, pp 275, 276.

71
Ervine, p 560.

72
Sandall, vol 1, p 281.

73
Because of its missionary character and traditional predilection for community service, The Salvation Army has tended to invest too much in outreach and not enough in the cultivation of the fellowship. In corps where this imbalance has persisted over a long period of time, the eventual result seems usually to be the loss of missionary vitality. Soldiery in mission who are not sustained, supported, nurtured and taught in the corps fellowship become weakened and succumb to mission burnout in one form or another. Increasingly, Salvationists are relearning for themselves that the Church's mission cannot be carried out effectively unless it *is,* in fact, the mission of the *Church*—an expression of the community of saints, which begets it, supports it, resources it, prays for it and provides a place of spiritual nurture, reflection and love for its leaders and workers.

74
James M. Gustafson, *Treasure in Earthen Vessels: The Church as a Human Community* (New York: Harper and Brothers, 1961), 'Time and Community: A Discussion', pp 113ff.

75
Gustafson derives these definitions from Wilhelm Dilthey, *Gesammelte Schriften*, vol 7 (Leipzig and Berlin, 1927).

76
The term 'dialogue' is used here not in the literal sense—although some preachers have literally dialogued with another preacher or the congregation in preaching—but in the figurative or imaginative sense to describe two-way preaching in which the preacher is projecting (imagining) interaction with the congregation in one form or another.

77
Thomas Oden, *The Intensive Group Experience: The New Pietism* (Philadelphia: The Westminster Press, 1972), builds a case for the crucial role played by small groups as supportive environments for spiritual formation throughout the history of the Church.

78
It should be pointed out, however, that a small group can itself become a vehicle for the reinforcement of prejudice. This happens when a group is formed for the purpose of protecting a prejudice or isolating members from the larger community. The best corrective for such tendencies in a congregation, of course, is the insistence that all groups be missionary or fit into the larger missionary plan.

79
See William A. Clebsch and Charles R. Jaekle, *Pastoral Care in Historical Perspective* (Englewood Cliffs, NJ: Prentice-Hall, Inc, 1964), for definition and development of these four functions in pastoral care practice during the history of the Christian Church.

80
This fact suggests a very important responsibility of the ordained minister or other designated person in the congregation: the *training* of lay shepherds.

81
The first of the Eleven Doctrines of The Salvation Army asserts that '. . . the Scriptures . . . *only* constitute the Divine rule of Christian faith and practice' (italic mine). The Scriptures, therefore, are the only source for authoritative guidance on the nature and use of spiritual gifts.

82
For this reason we recommend that each group in the congregation have a permanent, built-in agenda item: calling each member to account for his continuing development and deployment of ministry gifts.

83
It is noteworthy that William Booth was so concerned that his officers cultivate and practise the art of shepherding their flock that he published an allegory of Salvationist pastoring: *A Good Shepherd: or, What a Salvation Army Captain Should Be* (Being a Shepherd's Letter to General Booth), London: The Salvation Army Book Stores, nd). Early on, then, there was the fear that officers might become so involved in other ecclesiastical duties that pastoring would be ignored.

84
'Eschatological' refers to the last or latter things (Greek *eschatos*). In the New Testament the *eschatos* of God's decisive saving action begins in Jesus Christ, who represents or brings God's *kairos* (opportune time for salvation) (2 Corinthians 6:2). But the duration of *kairos* has not yet been exhausted. The saving opportunity will end in the last days which will herald the approach of the last day in which Christ shall be finally revealed (Matthew 24:3-14; Luke 1:33; John 6:40; 1 Corinthians 15; 1 Peter 1:3-5; Revelation 22:13).

85
Quoted from a letter written by Commissioner Tucker, 1 February 1902, from National Headquarters in New York City.

86
A 'gnostic type of salvation' is a doctrine of salvation based upon the gnostic assumption that spirit is good and matter evil. From this assumption one reasons that salvation consists of freeing oneself from bondage to matter by discovering the knowledge—*gnosis* in Greek means 'knowledge'—through which one can move toward a higher order of existence (ie, less tied to the material) and eventually to pure spiritual bliss and perfection. This view had gained a powerful foothold in the Mediterranean world in the time of the early Church, and in fact there are some passages in the New Testament which seem aimed at combating its insidious threat to Christian faith and practice. In the prologue to his gospel, John affirms the Incarnation (1:14), and in his letters asserts that those who do not believe that Jesus Christ has come in the flesh are not of God (1 John 4:2, 3; 2 John 7). The very idea of God's Incarnation—ie, the intentional union of perfect spirit and that which was, in their view, inherently evil (matter)—was unthinkable to gnostics. In his letter to the Colossians, Paul launches a frontal attack on gnostic views which were threatening to infect the church there in matters of both doctrine and practice. He affirms that the fullness of God did indeed dwell in Jesus (1:19; 2:9); that through the agency of God's perfect Son *all* things, including matter, were created (1:16); that rejection of the material as evil (extreme asceticism) as the only way of dealing with temptations of the flesh is seriously misguided (2: 16-23);

that going to the other extreme by indulging the flesh as that which is inferior and therefore can have no effect on one's spirit, is equally misguided (3:5); and that salvation in Christ is not for a small élite who can attain the keys or secrets to saving knowledge (gnosis) but rather is actually made available to *all* men (1:27, 28).

Hence, gnosticism disparages the place of the material in human existence, and a gnostic view of salvation is élitist and therefore incompatible with universal salvation in Christ. This means that a view of salvation for the poor that offers only postponement of hope (they are not considered part of the spiritual élite) and that does not deal hopefully with their existence in the world (they should recognise that matter does not matter) is throughly gnostic and contrary to the gospel.

87
This scheme for social salvation was developed in William Booth's, *In Darkest England and the Way Out* (New York: Funk and Wagnalls, 1890).

88
Quoted by Bramwell Booth in *These Fifty Years* (London: Cassell and Co Ltd, 1929), p 46.

89
All ecclesiastical discipline should be understood and evaluated in relation to the freedom that is in Christ and to the future to which God calls his Church. When Salvationists, for example, discipline themselves to abstain from substance abuse as well as from any use of alcohol and drugs, they are not condemning the mild use of alcohol and tobacco by some Christians; rather, they are undergoing a discipline to eliminate impediments to the best possible stewardship of the future. Drugs produce diversion from reality and escape from pain, leading often to sinful delusion, and eventually to self-destruction. Hence, abstinence can be pursued as an effective means of fostering positive movement toward God's future, avoiding certain pitfalls to pilgrimage, and encouraging others who are tempted to be diverted. (It is only fair to note, however, that there are other forms of substance abuse which deter from serious commitment of the body to God's future—for example, over-eating and caffein abuse. Salvationists have been strangely silent on these two.)

90
The term 'poor' is used here to refer to those people in a society who suffer from severe social and economic debility and comprise that part of the population which is most powerless against the vagaries of the

economic system and most susceptible to its ill effects. They are those whose health, well-being and security are most uncertain from day to day.

91
We are not naïvely suggesting that the poor should feel at home in every local congregation. The distinctive social and cultural character of specific congregations is a reality that ought not to be disparaged of itself. Rather, it can be looked upon as an asset for communicating with and offering community to persons of like background and orientation. What we are saying is indispensable to the congregation whose life and mission are based upon the gospel is both strong support of mission to the poor and sincere commitment to universal fellowship in Christ by making the outcast welcome and endorsing the Church's diverse cultural expression.

92
Michael Green, *Evangelism in the Early Church* (Grand Rapids: Eerdmans, 1970), pp 44, 45.

93
See Inglis, which deals with the Victorian churches' social and economic discrimination against the working classes. The pew system, for example, was one glaring form of this discrimination (pp 49ff).

94
Letter quoted in Frederick Booth-Tucker, *The Life of Catherine Booth*, 2 vols (New York and Chicago: Fleming H. Revell Co, 1892), 1 vol, pp 36, 37.

95
Sandall, vol 1, p 137.

96
William Hamilton Nelson, *Blood and Fire: General William Booth* (NY, The Century Co, 1929), p 173.

97
In 1875, three years before it was to become The Salvation Army in name, The Christian Mission wrote the following into its Foundation Deed:

> Nothing shall authorise the Conference to take any course whereby the right of females to be employed as evangelists or class leaders shall be impeded or destroyed or which shall render females ineligible for any office or deny them the right to speak and vote at all or any official meetings of which they may be members.

98
Catherine Booth, *Female Ministry,* pamphlet, 1859.

99
From letter dated 24 February 1890.

100
In utilising children as models of openness and trust, humility and honesty, understanding and insight, we are not suggesting the idealisation of pre-adulthood. Children *can* be dogmatic, suspicious, imperious, dishonest and very conditioned in their thinking. But we hold that these negative characteristics are learned or produced by conditioning from the adult world which inevitably, it seems, visits its sins and sinful dispositions upon the children.

101
In emphasising what children have to teach adults, we are not at all questioning the importance of Christian education for children in the Church. Rather, we are pointing out that adults in the Church also need Christian education, that a significant part of that education is the unlearning of acquired worldly outlooks that are contradictory to the Kingdom, and that children have an important role to play in providing refreshing outlooks that call prevailing world views into question. The Church, however, does have a crucial responsibility to teach and help the developing person to articulate and apply Christian faith. With the child, however, there is likely to be much less to *un*learn and much more intuitive faith to build on.

102
William Booth, *Training of Children*; or, How to Make the Children into Saints and Soldiers of Jesus Christ (London: The Salvation Army Book Stores, 1884), p 170.

103
Ibid, p 181.

104
By 'structure' we mean the forms and patterns by which the Church lives its life and carries out its tasks. This includes church government, rituals, the decision-making process, procedures and programme.

105
The special celebrations we have in mind here range from the Lord's supper and the love feast . . . to the recognition of Sunday-school

teachers. They include: baptism, enrolment of soldiers, dedication of infants, commissioning of local officers and other events that do not occur in every worship service. It is important that these celebrations should not be seen and carried out as independent observances that are unrelated to the focus and progress of worship. They should rather be observed as concrete expressions of the ways in which the Kingdom celebrated in worship is being received and God's future embraced.

106
Echoes and Memories, p 67.